THE
MAGIC OF
MONEY ALCHEMY

HOW TO REVEAL, HEAL AND
TRANSFORM YOUR RELATIONSHIP WITH MONEY

ELOISE BURTON

COPYRIGHT

Title: The Magic of Money: Reveal, Heal And Transform Your Relationship With Money

"THE ENERGY OF MONEY IS
BEAUTIFUL AND PLAYFUL."

ESSENCE & ENERGY OF MONEY CARDS

CONTENTS

INTRODUCTION

ABOUT ME

I'm a pretty normal, yet outrageously different kind of person. I know if you're reading this, that will likely resonate with you.

I don't come from money. I grew up surrounded by poverty. We didn't even have a car until I was 13. I only ever had one family holiday. It was normal. I didn't feel like I was missing out in any way.

As I grew older, I wasn't aware of money, other than it was scarce and hard. It came, it went and if I had any feelings toward it, it was a feeling of annoyance that it was even needed at all.

I started my working life doing a few factory jobs in my late teens and then realised that I wanted more than what was on offer to me. I didn't know what, but I knew I had to leave the town I was in to make the change, whatever that was.

So, I joined the Royal Navy and served for five years. After that I fell into, what I call 'people work': human resources, then training, then teaching in a college. I loved seeing people grow and develop and I noticed that not all training and education was good. I developed a fascination for quality of learning and built a career from this. Ensuring that what people were being taught was meeting great standards. I never thought I'd be interested in quality assurance as a kid, but I loved it.

I found I had a really good sense of what was working and what wasn't. I was often asked 'how do you do that' and in all honesty, I couldn't tell them. 'I just know/feel/see', it isn't something logical. Of course, I know now that it was my intuition.

I've had a few businesses over the years. I had the sense I was meant to do something, but didn't know what. So, I set up 'side hustles' and had huge success each time I did. But I also shut down each of the successful businesses.

Why?

I didn't know at the time, but I do now. I had some serious issues with money, and that impacted my feelings of self-worth, deserving and ability to receive success. I know that may sound odd, but also very familiar to you.

Once I saw this for what it was, I started learning about money mindset. It made sense, but I felt like it was lacking something. As I learned and grew, I (unknowingly) channelled the process and the phrase *money alchemy*. When I started reading about alchemy, I was astounded by how similar my process was.

I had never experienced channelling before. At least I thought I hadn't. When I explained to a friend how this idea had come to me, she pointed out 'that's channelling'. I have channelled many more ideas since and have really learned to trust this. It may not look or feel like standard channelling, if there even is such a thing, but it has never let me down.

Throughout this time, I have grown my income beyond my own belief. It's not where I'd love for it to be, but it is heading in that direction very fast.

My goal is to share the magic, and the logic of Money Alchemy, in a way that creates a deep connection with self and the world. I truly and sincerely believe that it is part of the shift that is occurring right now in our society.

As a person, I'm a super bubbly, big energy introvert. I love people, and I also need a lot of time for just me and my favourite things (crystals, cards and essential oils).

I have three weird and wonderful black cats and live with my partner Mark and my son Cam, who is now 22 and saving for his first house.

I'm not at all flashy when it comes to money. I drive a tiny little car and live in what most people might think of as a modest house, but it's my dream home and I love it. I rarely brush my hair or wear makeup. I am what is called an empath, a light worker, a teacher, a healer and a witch. 'The Money Alchemist' incorporates all of that perfectly.

Money has taught me so much about myself and about others. It's enabled me to be who I truly am. I don't need to act or behave in any other way. This is my favourite side effect of working with money alchemy. That I get to be my true self and feel great about it.

WHAT IS THIS BOOK ABOUT?

This book is about the magic of money and how it is easy to manifest, create, generate, earn, receive and be gifted more of it. Without working harder. Without doubting your worth. Without feeling guilty. Without being constrained by what others or society say you can't or should do instead. You can have the impact you want to make on your life, on your family, friends, community and the world.

The tried and tested ways which keep us stuck on the hamster wheel, the cycle of self-doubt, the illusion that you have to play small as a woman, for a million and one reasons.

As women, we are powerful! We may have forgotten this or hidden it, but it's still there.

Money and self, is a relationship that is often toxic. It's been used to abuse and control women since it was created and this continues today.

Stepping into a new way of being with money, will change *everything* for you.

WHY DID I WRITE THIS BOOK?

To inspire, give hope and create transformation. To show women not just how to connect with money in a beautiful and supportive way, but to help them remember their powerful magic that has been held down for so long.

We are the healers, the oracles, the creatrixes, the witches, the priestesses, the channels. Many of us have forgotten this.

As girls, many of us feel a purpose — even if you don't know what it is — you know you are here for a big reason.

Money is a magical tool for the powerful work we are here to do.

The sad thing is that we struggle to believe that we deserve money. We are talked down to and judged so much it makes us scared to even try.

Those who do try feel exposed, greedy and like they are doing something wrong.

This book was written so you can remember: You are worthy. You are worthy right now. You have always been worthy. You will always be worthy... of having everything in abundance, especially when it comes to money. Money can show you this, fast.

WHO IS THIS BOOK FOR?

I use the word 'women' a lot because it paints a mental picture for myself and others, although the approach outlined in this book will work for anyone, regardless of gender identity, but who can identify with the feminine energies.

Those who are ready to take a step into their power and create an impact. Those who suffer from fear and doubt around their self-worth.

Those who struggle to attract the money they deserve, not because they aren't good at what they do, but because they doubt themselves.

Those who believe or have been told they are terrible with money and can't be trusted with it. Those who have had proof, all their lives, that money is hard.

Those who have tried different ways of attracting and manifesting money with limited or inconsistent levels of success. Those who have been hurt by or with money in the past. Those who feel a call to something more inside, aching to come out but are stuck due to a lack of confidence

Those with jobs. Those with businesses or side hustles that they daren't call a business. Those with both. Or neither.

All who are open to something different. Those who are ready to embrace not just more money, but more love for themselves, as this is the primary side effect of this groundbreaking approach.

This book is for you!

WHAT THIS BOOK COVERS

In Part I, we'll go through some of the challenges and issues around money and how it affects you on an extremely deep level. A level you might not yet even be aware of. You start to see how the stories that have been created around money permeate every part of your being. At times you may feel triggered or annoyed as the truth reveals itself. Use this to fuel your desire to heal and transform your relationship with money.

In Part II, I introduce, in depth, the *money magic foundations* and how you can use them. These five foundations are the centre of my money alchemy process and something you'll return to over and over. Not only do they connect you with money in a truly empowering and fun way, but the foundations show you how to open your heart and soul to money in practical ways, which have a truly magical outcome.

Part III is a collection of musings and suggestions for action that will heal your money past and present and transform your money future. Some will feel familiar, this is a remembering after all. Others will be what my group call 'mic drop' moments and they'll be different for everyone. Take what resonates and leave what doesn't, and remember what you uncover and learn about yourself.

Throughout the book there are also statements relating to money. Many of them are from my Essence & Energy of Money card deck (see the Resources section for more details), others I've developed since creating the deck. They are designed to inspire a feeling in you. As you read them, notice if it's a positive or negative feeling. Negative feelings indicate that there is some work to be done specifically around that phrase for you.

WHAT'S IN THIS BOOK FOR YOU?

Imagine what it would be like to never worry about money… to never wake up in the middle of the night in a panic about it. Imagine being able to increase your income whenever you wanted to so you could have the impact you knew you were here to make.

Imagine feeling truly worthy, feeling connected to yourself and confident. Imagine never having to give anything from your 'cup', except the overflow.

How would that feel? That's what will happen if you apply the concepts in this book.

HOW TO USE THIS BOOK

This book can be used as you feel drawn to use it. I'm a dipper when it comes to books, so I've created this book in such a way that you can read it from cover to cover or dip in and out of it, as you want to.

Individually, the chapters will gift you something very powerful. In combination, you have the tools to totally change not only your life, but that of others too.

Each chapter has an overview and a summary of key points, so if you're in a rush, or aren't sure what you need, you can get a feel of the chapter before you dive in.

Some chapters may even repel you. This is very common when you work on your money relationship. That's ok. This is a sign that you need those chapters more than others, but you may not feel ready to face it. Keep coming back to it.

This is exciting and transformational work and at times I've found myself trying to learn everything all at once. If you start to feel overwhelmed, just put the book down for a few days then come back. Part of the healing process is time, and we often forget this.

Above all, use this book with an open heart. As you'll find out, money is a beautiful, high vibration being and this will ensure you get all the information you need to match this.

LET'S GET STARTED!

Are you ready to remember? As we journey through this book together, you'll become aware that you've seen this 'light' before. A long time ago. It will feel both familiar and completely new at the same time.

Money is a journey and Money Alchemy is the map. Like all maps, it is not the territory. There will be uncharted dips and hills, maybe even caverns and mountains.

You'll notice your mind, body and soul responding in different ways to different chapters for very different reasons, and this is part of the journey too. What you struggle with, will show you what you need the most.

Your beliefs will solidify and dissolve as you journey, as they do for me. This is part of the alchemy of this work. The important thing is to keep going.

You are about to embark on a journey into money, not as something you can touch, but as something you can feel in every fibre of your being. You're about to rekindle a beautiful and powerful relationship with your self-worth.

This information and connection will transform every part of you and bring back something you'd forgotten you could have.

I am here with you every step of the way...

Are you ready?

PART I
WOMEN AND MONEY

"YOUR MONEY HISTORY DOES NOT HAVE
TO BE YOUR MONEY FUTURE."

In this part of the book, several concepts, some old, some new, are introduced. Let's take a look at how society and our own experiences have affected our relationship with money and how this shows up in our lives.

Money is something that has been hidden away. I was told that it's vulgar to talk about money. That leads to some real, deep misunderstandings about money and creates a fear of it.

Let's explore those...

1: WOMEN ARE STILL QUITE NEW TO MONEY

> In this chapter, I'll explain a very brief history of money and women and shine a light on why it can feel like you aren't quite sure about it.

Women haven't had the right to their own money for very long, in the grand scheme of things.

Money has been around for over 5,000 years. There's been many different systems and approaches. When I first started down the amazing money rabbit hole, I looked into the history of money and women and was absolutely gobsmacked by what I found.

I'd always thought I should have been better with money, like somehow, I should have it all figured out. But when I realised that women haven't had money for very long at all, I felt a wave of relief rush over me.

Here in the UK, women weren't even allowed to open a bank account in their own name until 1975. Yep, you read that right. At the time of printing, that's less than 50 years ago.

The Sex Discrimination Act came into force in that year, which meant that women could no longer be refused a loan, on the grounds that they were female. The US was slightly ahead by a year or two. Even up until 1982, UK law meant that women couldn't even use their money to buy a drink in a pub.

Money is very, very new to women. And you know what? We're smashing it!

There aren't many role models of women with money — they are still the exception rather than the norm.

So, it then makes a huge amount of sense that there aren't that many women who have accumulated a huge amount of wealth.

Add on the fact that we often feel guilty for even thinking about wanting more money, it's still very rare to find a female role model when it comes to money and wealth.

Of course, there are some now, and I just want to reiterate just how fast they've done this: less than fifty years ago, money was not really in the hands of women.

Did you know, in 2022, there were 2668 billionaires in the world. Only 328 of those were women. Of those 328 women, two thirds inherited their money and one third are self-made, according to Forbes.com.

- Oprah Winfrey — TV host and author
- Kim Kardashian — reality TV star and businesswoman
- Rihanna — singer
- Sara Blakely — creator of Spanx

CHAPTER SUMMARY

- Money is still very new to women.
- Bank accounts have only become available to women in very recent history.
- Only a very small proportion of women are considered wealthy in their own right.
- Wealthy role models are still quite rare.
- Women are smashing it when it comes to money.

"MONEY TAKES ON THE ENERGY YOU GIVE IT."

2: MONEY AND CONTROL

In this chapter, I will touch on how money has been and continues to be used in a negative way and how this creates fear in you and others.

Money has been used as a control mechanism throughout history. For all, but especially for women. Often, we are held against our will in relationships, jobs and situations for fear of not having enough money to make a different choice.

Even abuse is covered up by money, to silence people or maybe even worse, to make them feel weirdly rewarded for allowing things to happen.

I had so much fear about leaving my first husband. He used money a lot to control me. Even to the point of making me feel useless when he was away at sea for months at a time, when our son was very young. I would have to ask him to transfer money to me whenever I could actually get hold of him (he was in the Royal Navy and we only got to speak a couple of times a month). He'd grill me on what I'd spent the last lot of money on. I had to justify what I needed to look after our son!

This got even worse after we split up. He refused to contribute at all because I left him. This created a massive feeling of vulnerability in me. I was never going to survive without him. And as a result, I did go back to him. He had complete control of me through money.

Shortly afterwards though, I realised that the relationship was mentally destroying me and this was not worth any amount of money, whatsoever.

I left and I survived. I even started to thrive.

My second husband used money to control in a very different way. He would buy me things to 'show me that he loved me' and that 'he was sorry' whenever there was a fall out. But often, I found I was criticised for not forgiving, just because an expensive gift was given.

He'd tell me he was a provider type which meant he didn't like the thought of his wife working full time. So, for many years I earned only a small salary, part time. I thought this was nice. Who doesn't like to be looked after? But I soon realised that this was a form of control too. Keeping me only earning part time, meant I had no escape again.

Leading up to the time we divorced, he dug us so deeply into debt, that I was beyond scared of leaving him. I stayed way beyond the point of no return and suffered very badly from depression and anxiety. I felt so trapped. He thought I could never bring myself to leave home. But I knew my son needed a mum who could show him a better way.

I've been advised not to take misogyny in the workplace further — aka 'your job/career will be impacted if you do'. I was even paid to keep quiet about bad behaviour in the workplace, when I left, because of discrimination. I bet you also have loads of examples of when money has been used to control you or others you know.

CHAPTER SUMMARY

- Money is still used to control.
- Crippling yourself with debt can often feel like the safer option.
- Misogyny and sexism perpetuate the feelings that money isn't safe or is used for bad things.

"MONEY IS A HUGE TABOO. LET'S CHANGE THIS."

3: SOCIETY AND MONEY

> In this chapter, I highlight how our society reinforces negative messages about money and creates shame.

Here, in the UK, we're taught from a very early age that it's rude or vulgar to discuss money. We simply don't talk about money other than 'I'm skint'.

In jobs, it's often written into contracts that you are not allowed to disclose your salary to colleagues and this has played a big role in re-inforcing shame and fear around money.

I bet you know more about your best friend's sex life than you do about their money life.

We're also taught that there's only one way to make more money: work harder, for longer.

There's a lot of shame around money too.

> **Some of the things I've been ashamed of when it comes to money:**
> - having a home repossessed
> - getting into £100,000 of credit card debt and not having a single clue what I bought with it
> - losing big chunks of cash because I was careless

- receiving money, I hadn't earned such as benefits, inheritances and gifts
- having debts that were written off — after all, I had used the money
- bouncing cheques
- needing to claim benefits
- staying in abusive relationships because of the money
- taking money to stay silent when I should have spoken out
- being conned at the Eiffel Tower into paying EUR 50 for a cheap plastic bird toy — what the heck!
- letting the use of money control me.

This money shame is crippling. It creates physical reactions in our bodies which sneak up, at the weirdest of times.

Other money shames my clients share:

- bankruptcy
- being the victim of fraud or theft
- being told they are no good with money or can't be trusted with it
- investing in themselves and not doing the work
- failed business attempts

CHAPTER SUMMARY

- Society tells us what to feel when it comes to money.
- Talking about money is frowned upon and this creates a lot of confusion and misinformation.
- Shame and money are closely linked.

"SHAME DIES WHEN STORIES ARE TOLD
IN SAFE PLACES"

ANN VOSKAMP

4: MONEY SHAMING

> In this chapter, I go even deeper into the shame that surrounds money, and how judgement is always present, whether you have money or not. I'll also look at some things you may have heard as a child that have manifested in a real confusion over what you are and what you aren't.

You may have heard of the term *money shaming* before, or maybe it's new, but you'll realise that not only have you seen it, you've probably done it yourself. I know I have.

Money shaming is being shamed for having money. This happens a lot in our society and it leads to you thinking things like 'it's greedy to want more', 'money will make me mean/spoiled, conceited/aloof etc etc'.

Here's the thing, you will be judged, and maybe even shamed. People with money are judged and shamed, and people without money are judged and shamed. No matter what you do, you will be judged and people will try to shame you.

Whether you are tall, or short. Whether you speak your mind, or do not. Whether you drive a flash car, or a little roller skate car like mine.

Women, in particular, get success-shamed a lot. It's one of the reasons I don't share my numbers very often. (Although I know I get judged for that too.) I'm still uncomfortable with being judged for my success.

And let me tell you... there are women out there who are far more successful than me, and they get judged and shamed.

You will never not be judged and this has been a very hard lesson for me. Family and friends have literally and figuratively walked away from me, or rudely and abruptly changed the subject, when my reply to "how's business?" is "amazing, I just had my best month ever".

I was shamed out of a clubhouse group of small, local businesses, because "no six figure business owners" were allowed, as, apparently, we are sleazy. I was told I was "too big for my boots" because I sent someone a booking link and didn't have availability for two weeks. I've been accused of trying to make money out of my spiritual gifts, which apparently, we're meant to give away for free. I've even had conversations end abruptly because people don't like that I talk about money positively.

It sucks being judged. However, you will always be judged by others. But, I definitely prefer being judged for my successes than my failures, many of which weren't in my control. So, my lovelies, knowing that you can never not be judged... shall we just go for it and just be flipping successful?

CHAPTER SUMMARY

- People will shame and judge you for just about anything.
- Having money, or not having money will result in judgement.
- As judgement is inevitable, let's get judged for being a success.

"WHAT IF I FAIL?
OH, BUT MY DARLING, WHAT IF YOU FLY?"

ERIN HANSON

5: FEAR OF FAILURE IS OFTEN FEAR OF SUCCESS

In this chapter, I explore the concept of the fear of success, which sounds completely mixed up. As you begin to understand the way the mind works, it will make much more sense than even the fear of failure.

Yep, you read that correctly. Often, we say (and believe) that we are afraid of failing, of looking silly, or making mistakes. But that stuff is well within your comfort zone. Trust me! We have been failing since the day we were born. It's how we learn, develop and grow.

It's how we learn to walk, talk, feed ourselves, go to the toilet etc. We fail! And when we fail, we learn. Or we fail again until we do.

I thought I was afraid of failure, having been humiliated for my short-comings in the past by various teachers, bosses, family members, friends and even an accountant.

But when I created my first business (selling flamingo and unicorn gifts) and it took off — it created so much pain, anxiety and even con-fusion in me; I had to step away from it. I even felt guilty for turning a profit within six months because a family member told me that no business makes a profit in the first five to six years.

You see, this was so far out of my comfort zone, my mind and my body just didn't know what to do. It felt unsafe to be successful. It felt like a fluke. Like maybe I'd done something illegal even.

So, I tried a different business. It took off even faster. This time I was selling sporting equipment on Amazon in the United States. It hit $100,000 turnover so fast that I freaked out yet again.

I tried to reason with myself. It was tipping literally thousands of dollars into my account every month and I was only doing about 10 minutes of work for it. It felt so wrong, even though that is "The Dream", right? What was wrong with me?

I shut it down, liquidated all the stock and went and hid for a while. It dawned on me at this point that success just made me feel very uncomfortable. Fearful even.

This was like a punch in the face — I'm scared of success?? That just didn't make any sense. But when I looked into this further, I realised this made absolute sense.

Your subconscious mind is designed to keep you safe and that means keeping you in your comfort zone. Here, in this squidgy, warm and safe space, your subconscious mind knows it's safe. When you take even a peek outside of this bubble of safety, you get all sorts of signals. Physical, mental, and emotional signals that yell 'whoa, don't do that, we don't know if it's safe.'

More on that later. But know this, fear of success is more common than you might think. More common than fear of failure. How has this shown up for you?

CHAPTER SUMMARY

- Your comfort zone is where your default is.
- Your mind attempts to get you back to the comfort zone.
- Fear of success is more real than fear of failure.
- Your mind is working beautifully for you, but might not be helping you towards your goals.

"MY MIND IS A POWERFUL TOOL FOR CREATING WEALTH."

ESSENCE & ENERGY OF MONEY CARDS

6: MONEY AS A WOMAN

In this chapter, I'll introduce you to a brand-new way of thinking about money. It will change everything and you will feel more connected than ever before with money.

From this point on, I invite you to think about money as a gorgeous feminine being. As a woman if that's easier?

Why? Money is not an energy as such, although many will challenge this. It's the vehicle we use to transport energy from one thing to another. And it will take on any kind of energy you put into it.

Have you ever had money given to you that felt icky because there were strings attached? That's money sent out with icky energy in it.

How about money that just felt joyful? That's money that's been sent out with joyful energy in it.

We're taught a lot of things about money that are negative and transactional, and when this happens we start using money with fear, anger, disappointment, annoyance and regret. These are heavy.

When you think about money as a feminine being, some gorgeous words come into play.

Money words:

- love
- flow
- create
- support
- nurture
- kind
- friendly
- peace
- calm
- ease
- grace
- inspire
- empathic
- feel
- gentle
- reflect
- fun

In my programs, we work with money as a gorgeous goddess. Sometimes she is golden, other times she appears as celebrities, deities, cartoons, or just a wonderful energy and more. Sometimes she even looks like money. But the difference is, when you connect with money as a feminine being, you instantly shift into a different feeling and vibration around it.

You start to see and feel money and bring it into your awareness more and more. As you build your relationship with this gorgeous feminine being, you learn more about her, and yourself. As the relationship deepens, she becomes a friend, and trust and faith arrive.

Now I know, if you haven't heard me talk about thinking of money as a goddess that becomes your friend, it might sound a little off the wall, but honestly, this different way of thinking and feeling about money will transform you.

Thinking about, and interacting with money in this way changes everything. Your relationship with her will change and evolve as you do. She's playful and creative and you might sometimes be surprised by how she appears to you over time. I've found that she always had profound and often surprising messages for me, (more on that in Part 2).

She will support you, shine a light on things when you are holding yourself back, give wonderful advice, and you will feel so much love in her presence.

Love was a word I had never associated positively with money before, but my goodness, this will change for you!

She is like a wonderfully close friend, whom I can trust to have my back and just the right message for me at any time.

The hardest thing about working with money in this way, is the resistance you will feel. The resistance, that 'I can't', or 'I don't have time' or 'I'm not in the right ...headspace'. That, right there, is your comfort zone screaming at you.

As I said, money will become a gorgeous friend to you, and just as with your other friends, your mind will convince you to avoid her when you know her approach is *exactly* what you need.

My friend and podcast co-host, Claire, for example, if I'm resisting something, my mind tells me 'You're too busy to meet with her', 'oops you forgot to text her again, too late now', even though she is the exact person I need to get me out of my funk.

This is what your mind will do with money too — the times when you resist connecting with her, are the times you need her the most. The easy times are, well, easy. But when it's hard it's even more important.

CHAPTER SUMMARY

- From this point on, think of money as a feminine being.
- Money isn't an energy, it's a vehicle for energy.
- Love and money feel the same when you take this approach.
- You'll find yourself avoiding this relationship, because it's good for you. Notice and get back on track.

"I AM A POWERFUL CREATOR AND MANIFESTER OF MONEY"

ESSENCE & ENERGY OF MONEY CARDS

7: MONEY & MAGIC

In this chapter, I share some more of my story and how I first discovered magic. Also, how money and magic collided for me and changed my life (and blew my brain a bit).

I can remember my magic and manifestation beginnings. From the age of five years old, I knew I had magic. Not the 'bippity boppity boo' kind, but a power to change things, to see things, to hear things and sense things that others either couldn't see or ignored.

For a while, I embraced it — as a child, you don't know any different right? But over time, I became ridiculed for my weird and crazy beliefs.

In my mid to late teens, I ended up in foster care, and my foster mother was a witch from Wales. I didn't know this at the time but I felt something powerful about her. I have such wonderful memories of her watching over me as I looked at, and fell into the tarot cards. Her super king cigarette used to burn all the way down, but she never flicked the ash, and it *never* fell despite her waving it around, while showing me how to protect my energy and see the spirits. In my smoking years, I tried and tried but never succeeded in doing this — it was her unique magic.

She rekindled my interest in developing my skills, but after leaving her care, I found myself surrounded by people who just thought I was crazy. It felt unsafe for me to have and practise these skills and I stuffed them down and became 'normal' (whatever that is). Normal was dull, it physically hurt me. I was 17 when I stuffed it back into that box it had been in before. When I look back at this time, I was so alone; I had my magic, but no one believed me. They all made fun of me and yet it hurt me to not use it.

After leaving foster care, I'd experience being on benefits and the shame that seems to come with that; even though it's assessed and judged that you can have it. I'd got in so much debt I didn't know what to do or who to talk to.

I was scared of money, and I hated it. It was everything that made life hard. Being in a damp flat that I couldn't afford to heat, in a concrete jungle estate, felt like rock bottom. I didn't want to think about it, and I certainly didn't feel like I was capable of having any, so I ran away and joined the Royal Navy. I knew there, no matter how hard money got, I'd have a warm bed and food.

This 'rock bottom' when it came to money became a repeating cycle in my life, and the pain of hiding my gifts still hurt, but I numbed it with depression. I felt like I was simply living to die. Like my wings had been cut off. I even attracted relationships, friendships and colleagues that perpetuated this feeling too.

The day I left my 2nd husband for the very last time was a pivotal moment in my life. A moment of sheer terror as the reality of my situation passed, not just through my head, but through my veins, like ice creeping slowly and steadily through them. I remember that moment like it happened just now.

My whole life stopped for what seemed like an age. Everything and everyone moved in slow motion. It felt like hours, but I know it was just a split second.

I saw all of the damage that suppressing my magic had done to me, and how in doing so had allowed others to hurt me in ways that even fiction writers couldn't think up. I saw how I had betrayed my intuition, over and over and over, and how this had really hurt me, mentally, emotionally and even physically. I saw how I'd neglected myself physically, emotionally, spiritually and financially.

I had nothing again, less than nothing in fact as the debt had just got bigger and bigger. But that was the moment I decided to live fully instead. To live as me, in all my glory.

I was physically sick after that moment passed. The first of many different energetic releases. As I reconnected with my intuition and magic, I became fascinated with manifestation. The film *The Secret* laid it all out clearly and I took notes and action. I wanted things to be different. I needed them to be different. Sometimes it worked, other times it didn't. I didn't understand.

Fast forward a few years and I met Mark. We wanted to buy a house together but it just was not possible. There was too much month left at the end of the money (i.e., the money runs out before payday). Even though we both had jobs that paid really well, there still wasn't enough money to get to the end of the month.

One day we were bored, so we went to see some gorgeous show homes, just to pass the time. I remember sitting in one near to us in Romsey Village. I remember the feel of the sofa as I sat on it and we worked out that if we saved for about 10 to 15 years, this house could be possible. At that moment we committed to making this our 10-year plan. We went home and I thought about all the things we could do to save some money. I looked at bank accounts and cancelled any direct debits that we didn't need. Reduced and saved on bills wherever we could. It resulted in a saving of about £200 a month. Not loads, but it was a start.

We realised that we were spending between £50 and £70 per week going for coffee and cake, so to save on that, we bought a bean to cup coffee machine. That was the start of something very magical. It got the ball rolling in terms of manifesting our dream house, because after that money just started raining down on us, in such a beautiful way.

We had money given to us as a gift, we had money returned to us from PPI refunds. Huge amounts of money that we just weren't expecting. We got bonuses, we got refunds and we managed to afford the deposit and get a mortgage on a house in a nearby town, within nine months. 10-15 years shrunk to just nine months!

What was really interesting about this manifestation of our dream house, was that we didn't even notice that we'd done it until maybe a year later. I was sitting in my office thinking and it dawned on me 'This is the house. This is the house that we sat in, in Romsey!' The same house, by the same developer, just on a different site.

A few years went by, and we fell out of the good money manifesting habits. Truth be told, I wasn't even sure how we'd done it.

This was almost six years prior to the time of writing this book, and in that time I've discovered something wonderful called Money Alchemy, which I'll explain in a while.

CHAPTER SUMMARY

- Magic was something I knew I had from an early age.
- The right person helped me nurture my magic.
- Like many others, I hid my magic to fit in.
- Money created the most amazing magic in my life.

"I MAGNETISE MONEY TOWARDS ME"

ESSENCE & ENERGY OF MONEY CARDS

8: THE SCIENCE BEHIND THE MAGIC OF MONEY

In this chapter, I very briefly touch on some of the science behind the magic of manifesting anything, but especially money. Each one is a rabbit hole in itself so you may want to do further research. For the purposes of this chapter, I have merely summarised some key elements.

Now, I love all the magical stuff when it comes to money. I come from a long line of healers and witches but I'm also very present on Earth at this time. My career, before I became The Money Alchemist, was in high level quality assurance of qualifications. A very logical, process driven role. Bet you weren't expecting that!

What's really interesting is that, even though I was doing a very logical job, there were several times that my boss would ask me 'How did you find that problem?' and I would simply say 'I just had a weird feeling'. It wasn't something I'd been trained to do, I just seemed to know where to look and it would appear.

If you've seen the film *Minority Report*, Tom Cruise has this screen on which he can move elements around and zoom in and zoom out. Whenever I went to quality assure somewhere, this is what I experienced, but inside my mind. I felt like I had that, like I could see things happening before they happened, so my magic and intuition never really left me It just evolved to help me be pretty good at my job.

As much as I enjoy having and using my magic and intuition, I love a bit of logic.

It's really important to me to have this, too. As in those times of doubt, or when I have lost faith, this is the stuff that reminds me that our magic is real. It may not be understood, but it is proven.

Intuition is one of many 'woo woo' things that scientists study. In fact, Dr David Hamilton has written a book called *Why Woo Woo Works: The Surprising Science Behind Meditation, Reiki, Crystals, and Other Alternative Practices*. This book is one I highly recommend if you have any doubt in your power to manifest, now or in the future.

The formula for which Einstein is famous for, $E=MC^2$, states that everything is energy. If everything is energy, then *we* are energy and energetic too.

Here are some interesting scientific things that confirm that we can change our situation through our intentions and energy.

1. MAGNETS

One of the first links to science I found, as I became more and more called to talk about money, was the idea of being a *money magnet*. That you can attract money as simply as a magnet can attract something that is magnetic. But this is only one side of the coin (pun intended) or the magnet. You see magnets have poles, and this means they can both attract and repel. So, in science you can be a magnet that repels. Changing a magnet's pole, by turning it, changes the energy field it projects — attract or repel.

2. ICE PARTICLES

In Japan, an experiment was carried out where a person would hold an intention or feeling whilst focusing on a glass of water. They found that when the water was frozen, it formed different shaped ice crystals depending on the feeling or intention that was given to it. So, you can change a physical reality with your feelings and intentions.

3. THE OBSERVER EFFECT — QUANTUM MECHANICS

Scientists have found that particles can be tricky. They change their behaviour based on the observer. It's thought that the intention of the person looking at it, impacts the way particles move. This means that what you focus on, you get.

So, there is proof out there, and there are many ways you can manifest money through energy and intention. There is a lot more to it though than willing your intention towards you and that's the part I think gets missed by manifesting gurus.

In the next chapter, I'll tell you more about money alchemy which adds in the missing bits.

CHAPTER SUMMARY

- There are many scientific studies that prove energy can be shifted.
- These studies show that you have an impact on the world you experience.
- You can attract or repel, just like a magnet.
- Money alchemy is the missing piece for manifesting.

"THE ACTIONS I TAKE CREATE PROSPERITY AND ABUNDANCE."

ESSENCE & ENERGY OF MONEY CARDS

9: MONEY ALCHEMY

In this chapter, I explain Money Alchemy®. Alchemy is a huge topic, so I've kept it very brief to outline the power and transformation it creates, rather than getting into the weeds of the 'how'. Money alchemy is the process I channelled shortly after I started working on my own money journey and it has proven to be a highly reliable and repeatable process which creates magic in your life.

I regularly get asked 'What is money alchemy?' and I need to start right at the beginning by first briefly explaining what alchemy is.

Alchemy is something you might have heard of. It's an old word that's often used by wizards and mages in TV and film. Have you heard of something called the 'philosopher's stone'? This is directly related to alchemy. It was believed to be the secret mix to turn lead into gold, as well as being the elixir of life.

Alchemy is often dismissed as 'hokum', but it was in fact the first form of chemistry as we know it today. So, again, actually quite scientific. It focuses on the transformation of matter, like metals, from one state to another; but also covers spiritual transformation too. It's a very detailed and specific process, but don't worry, you don't need to understand it to experience it. That is the joy of this work. It will work anyway.

'So, what is money alchemy, Eloise?' Money alchemy is quite simply the process of transforming from lack to abundance. It really is a simple process. Sometimes it's easy, other times it can feel a bit harder, but the more you use it the better you become at it, as with anything.

Back in my youth, when I was trying to manifest money and getting really inconsistent results, I didn't realise that I needed to heal to be able to manifest accurately and reliably. I was manifesting from a pretty negative place. Even though I had consciously managed to be fairly positive, subconscious beliefs were misaligned with conscious beliefs. No one can manifest well with this type of conflict.

This is why so many women tell me that when they've tried manifesting before sometimes it worked, other times it didn't. This causes you to lose faith in the process.

1. REVEAL

The first part of money alchemy is to reveal the blocks, stories, beliefs and patterns that are holding you back.

This stage can feel uncomfortable as you challenge things you have held onto all your life, and maybe even from past lives. You start to see things that you thought were fact as being partially or even fully untrue. Some of these discoveries will feel obvious and you'll be surprised that you even had them, let alone where they came from.

Others will be lurking in the shadows, hiding and hard to see, but the more you look the more will be revealed.

Even this stage on its own can have a profound effect on your manifesting abilities, but when combined with the next two, what you can create is really magical.

2. HEAL

Healing can take many different forms. It can be simple and fast, or it can be more challenging and progressive. But, one thing I can whole-heartedly promise you is *it is always worth it*. Healing can mean different things for different people. In money alchemy it can take the form of forgiveness, journaling, self-love, tapping, meditation, burning items or/and mental and physical releases (more on this later).

Imagine that in the reveal stage you spotted a belief that you wanted to change. The healing stage is about removing that, changing that and making sure that what is left, is healthy and won't reopen.

3. TRANSFORM

In this stage you notice things happening. It could be that sales are just more effortless; that you don't go bright red when you talk about fees. It could even be that you actually find yourself liking money and so much more. This is the shift to a new level of abundance.

Now, I wish I could tell you this is a 'once and done' process. But it's not. However, it is a process you can repeat and get even more abundance with every go.

What's even more wonderful about money alchemy, is that it doesn't just impact your manifesting abilities, it also impacts your relationship with yourself in such a wonderful way.

CHAPTER SUMMARY

- Money alchemy is based on the old science of alchemy.
- There are three stages in money alchemy: reveal, heal and transform.
- Money alchemy is a repeatable and reliable process.
- It is a process that you need to go through again and again, so you can achieve more and more abundance.

"MONEY DOESN'T ALWAYS LOOK LIKE NOTES, COINS OR NUMBERS IN MY ACCOUNT."

ESSENCE & ENERGY OF MONEY CARDS

10: MONEY IS ALCHEMY

In this chapter, I show you how to see the magic and science of money all around you, every day. Money is the ultimate alchemy but we forget to notice it.

Alchemy is about transformation and money does this all the time. It's my favourite thing to observe. We have lost the ability to see it though. But not for much longer. Simply by reading this, you'll start to notice it everywhere.

Think about it — you go to work, or run a business. This alchemises (transforms) into money. That money then alchemises (transforms) into the things you buy with it: food, electricity, internet, books, clothes, holidays, lottery tickets. Any time you change money into something else it is transforming.

It can even transform back into money! Imagine you bought a table, or a car, or a house even. When you sell it, it alchemises again into money. Sometimes into more money, other times into less, but back into money it transforms. You then use that money and transform it into something else again.

In fact, I think that everything that is man-made in our world is evidence of money being alchemy. Second only to our magical mother nature. Think about how any one of the walls of your home was once money. That money was transformed into materials to build and finish that wall. Perhaps you have some art on that wall that you created. Money transformed into the materials to create that, and you could even sell it, to transform it back into money. I love this concept so much, and it's very, very real.

Observe this in your life. Isn't it fascinating!

CHAPTER SUMMARY

- Money is transforming (alchemising) all around you, every day.
- Everything man-made has some form of money in it and can even been transformed back into money.
- Money is the ultimate alchemy.

"MONEY FLOWS TO ME WITH EASE AND GRACE"

ESSENCE & ENERGY OF MONEY CARDS

11: MONEY IS THE EASIEST THING TO MANIFEST

In this chapter, I look at why it often feels that money is the hardest thing to manifest, when it is actually the simplest, easiest and often the fastest thing to draw into your life.

You may feel like this chapter title just isn't true, but I promise you, it really is.

Many things we attempt to manifest have a lot of moving parts. Think about it, if you are working towards manifesting the perfect partner; they need to be located and meet your desires and be available and be where you are, whether that's physically or online, at the perfect time and in the perfect state. They also need to be ready.

Money is all around us so all you have to do is either see it, or take the opportunity or path the Universe presents for you to follow to the 'pot of gold'. This is often where it falls down. You might believe there is no money around you or any useful opportunities to gain it, and as a result you ignore it.

Often the easiest way to manifest money is to simply sell something, but this creates so much resistance in your mind and even your body that you'll do everything to avoid it. How do I know this? Because it happens to me, even now.

Noticing this resistance is powerful and will definitely help you to overcome it. Basically, if you procrastinate in any way you are resisting doing something. So, use this as your cue to notice what it is you might be avoiding and why.

Some of the first manifesting magic that women learn is the Parking Angel. If you haven't heard of this, it's when you ask the Universe or Parking Angel to create the perfect parking space for you. This works even in a busy city and you can often get a parking space right outside where you want to go.

This is another example of manifestations that have a lot of moving parts. Think about what your angel has to move and manage to get you the perfect spot right outside the shop you want to go to, at the perfect time for you.

Often this type of manifestation is described as luck, but it isn't. You intended it to happen and it happened. This is quite complex.

So, why does manifesting money feel sooooo hard, even though it is far less complex?

Well, not getting the parking space isn't going to have a huge impact on your life. You don't need it to survive, and it doesn't really mean anything if it isn't there. It's annoying and inconvenient, but you're unlikely to have long held beliefs about what it means to have it or not have it.

Quite simply, the Universe has a clear path, with no resistance, to send you this parking space. Put money into the mix and we have all sorts of resistance on the path to get to you, even though it's right there. We attach emotions to money that cause us to not even see it when it is in plain sight.

We have all these rules about the way money has to come to us, such as through hard work. We struggle to receive it, even if it does arrive and this means that often, you'll need to manifest ways to get the money that you aren't even aware of.

Ever got a nice chunk of money unexpectedly, just to have a car repair, tax bill, washing machine breakdown or some other issues happen?

And guess what? The amount it costs to put it right is almost the exact amount you managed to manifest.

We push money away from us. We stop it coming to us, and if it does get to us, we get rid of it, unknowingly and fast. Sound familiar?

CHAPTER SUMMARY

- Our feelings and beliefs about money mean we push it away.
- Manifesting money has way fewer 'moving parts' than other manifestations.
- Letting go of the meaning is what is needed.
- You'll have some conscious rules about where money can come from.

"MONEY IS IMPORTANT AND GOOD"

ESSENCE & ENERGY OF MONEY CARDS

12: MONEY AND YOUR MIND

In this chapter, I'll be looking at just some of the unconscious blocks you create to keep money from coming to you, or staying with you. The list is endless but identifying these is the vast majority of the work.

Having read to this point, you will probably be starting to think about some of the ways you've unknowingly managed to block attracting money to you. First off, there's nothing wrong with you for doing this. It's something we've been taught to do in so many ways.

Your mind is amazing. If your mind has a story about something being bad or unsafe, regardless of whether it makes sense, it will protect you from it. Most people have learned that money is something that could hurt us, even though, logically, it can also help us. So, your mind is doing exactly what it has been programmed to do… keeping you safe.

Money blocks, stories, beliefs and patterns exist in most of us but how can we know for sure? Well, there are symptoms of these things.

Often, the first symptom people notice when they start working with money alchemy is a feeling of being triggered. This isn't just a thought, it's also a feeling and sometimes even a physical movement. I often see things such as folded arms, eye rolls, shoulder slumps and sucked in lips. I liken it to your inner child having a bit of strop or tantrum.

Very powerful words also fall out of peoples' mouths when they are triggered by money. My favourite so far has to be 'that's preposterous'. Others include 'impossible', 'insane' and 'it can't be done'. All of these words indicate a very firmly shut door when it comes to opening up to even dreaming about money.

What I love most about this work is how fast those doors open, just a crack, then a bit more, and before long they are off the hinges. What door?

These are not made up though. Those words and reactions are genuine and they come from a deep place. You'll even have proof to support your block too. You will even have seen what seems like the universe telling you not to do things, by putting obstacles in your path.

When you start manifesting more money into your life, you're going to see more and more of these blocks coming to life. I still have them today. For example, every time I create 'bigger' money in my life I start arguing with Mark. Generally, we don't argue as a couple, but when I get close to that block we start arguing. It feels real because it is real: but once you've seen it as a block, you have more understanding of it.

I think it's important to separate our subconscious and unconscious minds here. Many of us have conscious goals to make more money and to be more successful. Consciously we are completely on board with these goals and aspirations, but somewhere in our subconscious, something prevents it happening and that is the block, story, belief or pattern.

Why do blocks like this occur? Your subconscious mind is working perfectly. If you have a money block, it is because your subconscious mind is designed to keep you safe. It's designed to keep you in your comfort zone and what that means is that anything that is new, feels unsafe.

The way that your subconscious mind tells you that, is by creating a triggering feeling or a gut feeling that's telling you 'You shouldn't do this, it's not right for you, you can't do this'. It gets really loud in there.

Fear of the unknown is extremely loud, until it's known. At that point, all that noise is nowhere to be found. Not even a pat on the back for doing it.

Beliefs, blocks, stories and patterns often form in times of trauma or in your childhood and they make absolutely perfect sense at the time they're created. For example, a really common phrase about money is that 'Money is The Root of All Evil'. Many are told this from a very early age, especially if you are brought up in a religious family.

There's no filter when you're a child or when you're in trauma. Therefore, your subconscious mind thinks it's completely logical for you to be afraid of money or to feel it's unsafe to have money, because it will make you evil or it will take you down the wrong path. Isn't that clever? It spots the danger signs and it stops you by steering you in a different direction.

I want you to take a moment to really feel some gratitude for your subconscious mind and how powerful and clever it has been for you.

Often these blocks have been there for a very long time and they made absolute sense when they were created. However, the future is not the past and the present is not the past. The only thing your subconscious mind can base any decision on, is the past, so it makes no sense to hold on to these blocks, stories or beliefs anymore.

When you start to clear them, you start to see more money coming towards you and that's both exciting and scary. When you heal the block, things change and you're experiencing it for the first time, but you get used to that very quickly. You'll start levelling up and before you know it, that block which was holding you back, holding you at a lower level, has gone and allowed you to rise up to another level.

I often get asked 'How do I know if I've got a money block?' Here's how: if you haven't got all the money you want in your life then you very likely have a money block.

Even people with lots of money can have money blocks. You often see people that seem to be really wealthy being quite mean with their money and that can be because they're afraid of losing it. That could be a money block that actually stops the money growing further.

Where you feel triggered is where the gold is. I know it sucks, but when you notice a reaction to a subconscious block, dig deeper. You will uncover some treasure. It's often hard to face it and it can feel scary facing your money blocks. When you see them, they might make you laugh, or maybe even cry. Sometimes it won't make any sense, but trust that it made perfect sense to your mind at the time it was created. Remember, your mind thinks it's keeping you safe by holding onto your belief. If you can shine a light on it, even for a moment, you will reduce the power that that block has had over you significantly. I often say that once you identify your blocks that's 80% of the work done. You will notice it every time it pops up and you will feel it and know what it is and just having that awareness is amazingly powerful.

Once you know it's just a money block you can work with it.

Don't beat yourself up for having these blocks, just remind yourself of how perfectly your mind is doing its job. It doesn't mean you have to continue with those blocks or beliefs though. Things change, you change, no moment in time is ever the same and so the belief can change too.

CHAPTER SUMMARY

- Your subconscious mind has the job of keeping you safe.
- That doesn't mean it can't be changed.
- What kept you safe before, might be hindering you now.
- Identifying these blocks is 80% of the work.
- You mind is marvellous — even if it has been overprotective.

"MONEY IS A HEALING JOURNEY."

13: GETTING YOUR MIND ON THE 'MONEY BUS'

In this chapter, I cover how to move past a block and onto the road to belief. It can be a little bumpy at times, but it is a conscious choice to do this. You'll need to make this choice over and over, but it will get easier as time goes on.

Your conscious mind is often screaming 'Yes, I'd love more money in my life.', while your subconscious mind is thinking that money is 'the root of all evil', 'it's vulgar', 'it will make you into a bad person'. So, how do you go about getting your subconscious mind on the bus, so to speak?

I truly believe that working with money is a healing process. I have certainly increased my connection with myself, my confidence, my self-esteem and rediscovered my worthiness through working with money. It's even had an impact on my physical being too. My anxiety levels are much more manageable and I no longer need medication to manage them. My sleep has improved and even my digestion is much better.

I'm not saying that working with money will heal all your ills, but I am saying that when you work on money, healing happens in many different ways. You will notice improvements in yourself that seem unrelated, but are actually part of the work. My doctor often asks me what I'm doing differently and really the only thing is money alchemy.

The more I grow and heal my relationship and connection to money, the healthier and happier I feel (see Chapter 25 for more on this).

There are many ways that you can heal money blocks, that can get your subconscious mind on the bus and I'm going to cover some of those in more depth in Part 3 of this book.

You can use all sorts of things to help you to heal your money blocks. You can use journaling, reiki, emotional freedom technique, hypnotherapy, rapid energy release, affirmations, visualisation, meditation and all sorts of healing practices to name but a few.

To get to the point of healing, you need to be 'on the bus'.

I heard this phrase during my career. It was used in an attempt to get people to understand and it made me both laugh and realise I had to choose whether to get on it.

You will often find you have got off the bus, without even realising it. This will be when you notice that money is getting harder again and that you aren't feeling that connection to money or self as strongly, or maybe even at all.

On the bus, is where the journey happens, where you move along, where you heal and where you grow.

Off the bus is where you get caught up in the old way of closing down to the idea of money being a free and feminine being and getting caught in the transaction, rather than embracing the flow. There's nothing wrong with this by the way. It is certainly the option I took for most of my adult life. I survived. I didn't starve. However, I find being on the money bus far more colourful and fun.

It gives me time to rest and time to think. It moves me forward.

That being said, I still jump off the bus. Sometimes I don't know why; other times, I'm a bit scared to go to the next place. Sometimes I do it knowingly, other times I notice it way after it's happened. Sales begin to slow down, money feels scarce and bills start landing on the door mat.

The most fantastic thing about the money bus is that as soon as you request it, it's there. There's no fee to jump on and you don't get punished or judged for getting off. Money welcomes you back on board with open arms and love, and you can take the next leg of your journey.

If you don't request the bus it won't arrive. Sometimes I resist doing the work, and that's ok. I think of this as a little break. Sometimes we need to get off the bus, to see where we are.

Doing things that are good for you, often feels like the hardest thing to do. This is because your subconscious mind will choose comfort over the unknown, even if the unknown is something wonderful. So, you have to make the choice to get on the bus.

Being on the bus is just a metaphor for 'doing the work'. When you feel resistance, look into why. There may be sneaky beliefs or blocks in there.

CHAPTER SUMMARY

- The money bus is a metaphor for doing the work.
- You have to make the choice to get on, over and over.
- There's no fare to pay, and no punishment for jumping off.
- When you're ready just get back on.

"I AM OPEN TO RECEIVE EVEN MORE GLORIOUS MONEY"

ESSENCE & ENERGY OF MONEY CARDS

14: ENERGETIC ZEROS

In this chapter, I start to explain the term *energetic zeros*. These are fascinating to me and I love working on them with myself and with clients. They are the physical manifestation of blocks and they can be really fun to work with.

I used to think that zero was, well zero. But over the years I've learned that when it comes to money, we all have four zeros, and they may not actually be zeros.

Confused? Let me explain... Over your lifetime, you will have had points with money that felt comfortable — even if in your mind they 'weren't right'.

Perhaps you have an overdraft of £2,000, and so long as you don't go over that limit you feel like money is ok. Not great, but not a disaster. Maybe you have a credit card which you pay off, then BANG! It's maxed out again in a short while. Or, if you started your business, did you get stuck at or around your previous salary level? These are energetic zeros.

It's where you subconsciously feel comfortable, even if you want to clear your debt or earn more. It can appear in savings too. You might find that whenever you go over a certain number, something happens and you end up right back at the number you were aiming to get past.

The four energetic zeros	
Debt	the amount of debt we are comfortable with
Buffer	day to day expense account
Savings	how much we can hold long term
Income	amount we can consistently generate

There's no specific order to these. You can work on all of them, some of them or one of them, and this will make a massive difference to you.

DEBT ENERGETIC ZERO

Here's my debt energetic zero story. When I was £100k in debt, I felt it. It felt heavy and hard, and I constantly worried about it. Over time, I paid more and more off, and it kept coming down. I got it down to £35k and then got stuck.

For about two years, it didn't seem to matter how much I paid off, the number would stay around £35k. I'd buy things, or need to pay bills and would end up right back at £35k again. What was happening?

£35k was my energetic zero — it was where I didn't love being but it was ok and felt manageable. To be fair, it was still a huge number and consciously I wanted it gone, but subconsciously I'd hit a sweet spot. When I realised this, I knew this was something I either could accept or change. I elected to change it.

Over time, I changed my energetic zero and it moved from £35k to £15k and the same thing happened again! I got stuck. But this time I worked out what it was and how to shift it.

Now my energetic debt zero is £500 and I'm really happy with that. I tried actual £0 with debt, but I found this very stressful. This shows me that there is more work to be done.

BUFFER ENERGETIC ZERO

A client came to me feeling stressed out that her day-to-day expenses were keeping her stuck in a struggle. She only ever seemed to have just enough. It didn't matter if she earned a bit more that month, it didn't seem to make any difference. It just got absorbed into the expenses.

Her energetic zero was actually zero. Consciously this was creating a lot of worry, but subconsciously, this was her sweet spot.

Her money personality meant that the thought of saving, felt dull and boring and 'what's the point'. Her belief that she could even do it, was just not there. So, I talked to her about creating a buffer. A small one to start with:

£500

Her goal? To always have £500 in her bank account, and if it went below that, get back to it as fast as possible. She had no idea how this was going to happen, but intention is a powerful tool and within a few short weeks she had done it.

This was someone who was struggling to get above zero, yet with a clear intention and bit of a challenge, she shifted into having and holding a minimum of £500 in her account. She felt lighter, her conscious fear reduced and she was amazed at how quickly her zero shifted. Today she has a much higher buffer in her account and holds that beautifully. It means that even when things go wrong, she has money. Then she just works to top it up.

The freedom this new energetic zero has given her has not just created more security, but has also affected her confidence and her ability to receive and hold even more money from even more sources.

Every now and then, she needs to use some, or even all of her buffer. But when she does, it fills up again almost magically. She is learning to unhook from 'the how' and allow her new energetic zero to be her new normal.

Just imagine what it would feel like to deal with most emergencies without over stretching yourself, or having to go even further into debt. What would that be like for you?

SAVING ENERGETIC ZERO

This can often be the last one people feel ready to work on. 'How can I have savings if I have debt?' is often the confusing part. And it's something I've struggled with too but you *can* have both, and I would recommend it.

Saving can feel scary — perhaps you've never had any before. Perhaps you're worried you'll just blow it all. Perhaps you don't feel like you can trust yourself. Saving is an investment in you — an investment in your future. And, lovely, you are worth investing in!

Think of your savings as your roots. They grow deeper and deeper every time you add to them, making the future more stable.

Now if you're thinking 'I can't think of anything more boring than saving', I get it. But if you give it a try, you'll see what I mean. When I started saving (and my saving energetic zero has been the biggest challenge for me) I felt like it was pointless. Like it was stretching me too much. I couldn't see it growing fast enough. But every time I added to it, I felt a touch of pride in myself. I knew my future self would thank me for it too. I slowly got a little addicted to that feeling and as a result, my savings increased a bit faster.

INCOME ENERGETIC ZERO

If you've been stuck at a certain level of income in your job, business or another form of income, it can feel like you're just not getting any traction. It's often referred to as a glass money ceiling. I call it an energetic zero.

When I first started out on my business journey, I found I was attracting almost the exact same amount as my salary before. Sometimes I would go over it one month and then the next month, go under it. It averaged out to my old salary. Maybe this was all I could make? Nope, this was just my zero.

I started using Magical Manifestation Cheques (see the chapter on these) and within a year I had tripled my income. I was blown away — that hallowed £10k a month was mine!

That in itself was fabulous, but over time, I realised that £10k a month was my new normal. That I rarely went below it, or over it. It always averaged out at £10k per month. It didn't feel much different to when I was generating under £3k a month either. It was just normal.

Interesting, eh? My new subconscious comfort zone with income had increased. Could I do it again? Yes!

Over the next two years I almost tripled it again. As I write this book, it's not yet consistent. I'm having some resistance, but I know it will settle and become my next new normal.

Guess what? It doesn't feel any different. Yes, things are easier and I can do more things and hire more people to help me, but I feel the same. Normal but safer.

CHAPTER SUMMARY

- There are four energetic zeros: debt, buffer, savings, income.
- These are limitations that are your blocks and beliefs manifested in this reality.
- Changing your energetic zeros will create a feeling of security and freedom.

"I RELEASE FEAR AND HATRED OF MONEY."

ESSENCE & ENERGY OF MONEY CARDS

15: MONEY WOUNDS

In this chapter, I go a bit deeper into some blocks that are actually wounds. These feel even more real than beliefs, patterns and stories because you can remember them so well. *Money wounds* are painful. They drain you of your self-worth in so many areas of your life, but like beliefs, they can be healed.

Did you know that money can actually cause wounds? Well, the way we use money and have it used against us can inflict wounds.

A money wound is a trauma or scar that was actually caused by money. Often, blocks, stories, beliefs and patterns are formed by other people, society and our own feelings of self-worth, or rather lack of it.

In addition to this, significant events caused by money or involving money, can create very specific and very painful blocks and stories. These lump on top of all the money 'junk' you already have and add clear and obvious proof of unhelpful things.

Money wounds examples:
- money is bad
- I can't be trusted with money
- money just hurts

Some examples of money wounds are having a home repossessed — like I did. This can be caused by all sorts of things: a loss of a job, a break up, a reduction in income, an increase in outgoings, even rising interest rates. This can be further compounded by the lowering of house prices which creates negative equity, making it almost impossible to sell instead.

For me, my home got repossessed because I couldn't face even looking at money. If I had, I genuinely think I could have stopped the action and maybe even still have that house today. On top of the trauma of having the repossession happen, I have guilt that I could likely have stopped it.

In addition to the immediate trauma, most cases of repossession end up with you owing a huge amount of money even though the house has been taken back. The mortgage companies rarely sell the properties for their full value and so you are left with no home and significant debt.

If that isn't enough, even renting a home becomes a challenge. A repossession decimates your credit rating. I couldn't even have a debit card after mine happened, and was forced to use just a cash card for many years.

My goodness, no wonder it's so traumatic!

There are other types of money trauma which are equally disturbing, if not even harder on us.

Types of money trauma:

- bankruptcy
- debt orders
- fraud
- bribery
- theft
- being bullied for being poor
- being bullied for being rich

I know several of my clients had their hard-earned money taken from them by their own parents. Often not because they were being mean but because they needed it to survive. This creates a feeling of money being unjust and unfair.

These money traumas create really sticky core beliefs about money. In fact, they don't just create beliefs, they create so many negative feelings, that it can become very challenging to see money positively and actually learn to trust it.

People often ask me if they manifested this negative situation. In a lot of cases, including mine, I think the honest answer is yes. When I look back over my life, I can see how my treatment of, and my relationship with money created this huge issue. However, oftentimes and nearly always to some degree, other people are involved who 'helped' you get to that state with money.

Some people are mean and take huge delight in hurting people — and this includes using money as their weapon of choice. We can't control that. But what we can do, is learn to change the vibrations we are sending out to attract these people and situations.

No one deliberately creates any of this for themselves, but there are things you can do to reduce the chances of it happening and the impact it has.

The number one thing that would have stopped my repossession? *Pay attention to your money*. I deliberately avoided this.

This Christmas, I did a live masterclass and reminded everyone who attended of this point. One of the lovelies who came shared that she had just checked, on the back of my reminder, and found that her card had been used fraudulently. She was worried that she had manifested this but I pointed out that this stuff does happen, and if she hadn't paid attention at that time, who knows how much would have been taken.

As a result of her paying attention, she caught it before her account was emptied and reported it to her bank who promptly returned her money and got it all sorted. Paying attention is a money magic foundation for a very good reason — if you aren't paying attention, you have no awareness. No awareness is what often gets us into situations that hurt us.

Having said that, the most important thing I learned to do after my repossession, was to forgive myself. Back then, I wasn't working with money as I am now. I punished myself for years with self-doubt and self-sabotage, over and over.

Money has already forgiven whatever you think your role, or lack of role was in this situation. She doesn't hold grudges. As a feminine being, money is unconditional in her wanting to be with you.

I wish someone had told me that. Forgiving myself was hard. I felt I couldn't trust myself with money and no one else should either. I created stories and beliefs about why I couldn't do things such as buy another house etc. But they were just stories — really believable ones, but they just weren't true.

I still had this money trauma when we manifested our house. It felt like I held my breath for what seemed like years while we waited for our mortgage offer. When we did get it, they were willing to give us way more than we needed and this scared me so much. 'I can't be trusted with that much money — I have proof!'

In all honesty, it's only since I started channelling money alchemy that I truly started to forgive myself. I wish I'd started this sooner. What's hard is that by forgiving a significant event in your life, it almost feels like it didn't matter. It had created all of the fear and chaos and yet it didn't mean anything if I forgave myself for it. I had just made a mistake and I'm moving on.

Our minds are beautiful, but also complex things. Often what we need to do is the hardest thing, even if we know it's the right thing to do. Money trauma creates deep wounds and scars, but they are healable. They often make more sense to our minds than some of the other types of blocks, stories and beliefs we have, as the cause is obvious.

There is another type of money trauma which I wasn't aware of until quite recently. Vows of Poverty. These are often taken in a previous life by our soul and brought into this life. They are actually quite common and link to many parts of our history, particularly that of women. These vows can be released, as with other types of money trauma, but can take some figuring out. I think of them as really complex knots, but once you have the thread, they can be released.

What makes money trauma so powerful, is that it creates cold, hard, proof that money is not safe for us to have. Unless you see it for what it is: something to be healed and released. Safety is a huge part of working with money. You might find yourself saying and even thinking that you want more money, but if somewhere in your subconscious there is even a hint of money not being safe for you, you will struggle to attract and keep more.

In the next chapter, I go a bit deeper into what makes us feel unsafe, and it may not be what you think.

CHAPTER SUMMARY

- Money wounds can be caused by trauma relating specifically to money.
- They create feelings of shame, anger and hurt.
- Vows from past lives are money wounds we bring into this life.
- Wounds have cold, hard proof for staying away from money.
- They can be healed.

"THE HISTORY OF OUR ANCESTORS STAYS WITH US,
ESPECIALLY WHEN IT COMES TO MONEY."

16: THE WITCH WOUND AND MONEY

In this chapter, I briefly introduce the *witch wound* and how it can impact you as a woman, here and now. This is a huge topic and it is included here to give some context to where a lot of your money 'stuff' may be linked to. It gives me goosebumps, even now.

When my clients come to me, they often aren't aware of the witch wound. It's something that we all carry. It was something that was learnt and passed through generation after generation. Some people also experience it as a past life. Some people feel it is very real in this life. Most will feel some connection to it, as I explain it some more. For me, my skin goes all goose bumpy and I feel sadness and anger for my sisters from that time. But I also sense that the witch wound is not the first collective trauma that we've experienced.

The very fact that women have not had access to their own money until fairly recently in history, makes me feel that there is something even more to this. There are many books and resources on the Witch Wound that will go into much more depth, but for this chapter I briefly explain what the Witch Wound is and how it impacts money and success.

In the Middle Ages, it was deemed to be something very evil and wrong to be considered a witch. But the people making the judgement didn't really know what a witch was and often people with healing gifts would be considered witches.

In her book *Witch* Lisa Lister explains that the word witch is derived from 'wicce' which translates as 'wise'. Not all witches were women, but most were. These were women who knew the magic of the Earth. They might have created potions like teas and tinctures (some of which we still use today). They would say healing chants and ward off evil spirits. They were the energy workers of their time. Often very gifted with intuition, some could see the past while others could see the future. Some could see illness in your aura. They were and are in tune with everything around them.

For some reason, there was a need to stop these wise women from healing and helping their villages. Women thought to be witches would be tested. In many cases this test involved a ducking stool being strapped to a stool, and then dunked in the pond or river. If they drowned they were considered to not be a witch, if they survived they were considered to be a witch and were burned.

Just have a read of that last sentence again. What do you notice? Regardless of whether they were deemed to be a witch or not, they were killed — one way or another. So that meant that even if you were simply being accused or thought of as a witch, it was deadly.

What I think was even harder about this time, and times before that have yet to be revealed to us, is that women were turned against each other. They were manipulated and threatened so they would give up the other women in their village. Often threats to their lives, or even worse, to their children, inspired the women to turn on each other. This created such a deep rift in the sisterhood and we still suffer from it today. At times it feels very lonely, doesn't it? You might have experienced, like me, that some of the friends I'd had did not actually have my best interests at heart. In fact, the opposite. It feels like such a raw and visceral betrayal, because of this wound. It teaches you to not want more, for fear of upsetting others and fear that they might turn on you.

I identify as a witch myself. I've always known I had gifts and a real connection that not everyone feels. I believe my own grandmother was condemned to an asylum for her gifts, but I'm unable to confirm this — no one ever spoke of her after she died.

For me, being a witch was just a part of who I am. We are called many things now. Empaths, intuitives, lightworkers, psychics etc. For me, it's an ability to see magic in our world every day. It's not always easy, but it is always magical. It's a big job too, waiting to heal and help people when they are ready. My special magic is money healing: money alchemy.

You don't need to be a witch to feel this. Many women feel it simply as part of their ancestral line, regardless of whether they identify as a witch themselves. This collective trauma means that it feels very unsafe to share our gifts and talents with the world. When we don't speak our voices or share our gifts, we aren't able to help people. Like me, I imagine you have felt called to help others throughout your life, in different ways, but if it feels unsafe to do so, then you're less likely to do it. This has a direct influence on your ability to manifest and attract more money.

CHAPTER SUMMARY

- The witch wound is a collective trauma.
- It is an example of history reaching into the present.
- The wounded feel scared of success and being visible.
- You don't need to be a witch to be affected by this.

"MONEY CREATES FREEDOM FOR ME."

ESSENCE & ENERGY OF MONEY CARDS

17: STEPPING INTO THE NEW WORLD OF WOMEN CREATING WEALTH

In this chapter, I open the curtain on our 'brave new world'. It sounds huge, and in a way, it is, but in another way it's very small and personal. This is for you, but it's also for the entire world, and everyone and everything in between. Exciting, eh?

I believe it's so important for women to connect with money in a more positive way. To create wealth for themselves and their families, so they can change the narrative around women not having money and being controlled by it.

Women who create more money do more and more wonderful things, and this creates ripples. Not just for now, but for future generations. Even healing ancestral lines and past life trauma. Including the very powerful and very real Witch Wound which I have previously shared.

Think for a moment... what would you do if you had more money?

I'm going to guess there's a lot of good you would do with it. Am I right?

I also want you to think about how it would feel to not feel scarcity. To have faith in your manifesting magic and be able to create and create and create more and more. And that it's easy.

Women becoming wealthy, whatever that means for you; be it a few hundred or a few billion and everything in between, is an unlearning, an undoing of centuries and millennia of conditioning, expectations, restrictions, society norms and unspoken rules around our worthiness to have money.

It's a reconnection with your soul, and a journey to return to your natural state of abundance which has been long forgotten.

It's a remembering of your true energy, and magic.

What would it mean for you to reconnect with all of that?

For me it's joy, peace, calm, serenity. Knowing I can trust myself 110% to manifest more and more and create a different present and future.

CHAPTER SUMMARY

- Having more money will create a positive outcome in the world.
- Women with money do wonderful things.
- This work ripples out to future generations.

PART II
THE MONEY MAGIC
FOUNDATIONS

When I channelled Money Alchemy I also received these gorgeous money magic foundations. My clients and I use these, and it creates such a shift, that it really can only be described as magical.

These are a great way to get back on the money bus (as described in Chapter 13), and act as an opening back up to abundance and a return to your journey.

"THERE ARE NO LIMITS TO THE MONEY
I CAN BRING INTO MY LIFE"

ESSENCE & ENERGY OF MONEY CARDS

18: INTRODUCING THE MONEY MAGIC FOUNDATIONS

In this chapter, I give a brief introduction to *money magic foundations*, what they are and how often to implement them. In the next chapters, we'll break down each one for you.

When money alchemy was delivered to me, through my higher self, The Universe or wherever it came from, it was complex. It still can be, but I'm exactly the right person to simplify it and make it a logical, yet still magical process for you.

Money Magic Foundation benefits:
- switch on your ability to see abundance
- create a light, playful feeling about your money relationship
- prioritise money and you
- connect you to a positive vibration around money

The five Money Magic Foundations are:
- Look for money
- Money loves attention
- Make space for money
- Speak kindly of money
- Money loves to be appreciated

Alchemy of any sort requires the repetition of transformation. And so, I knew that there needed to be some clear and foundational steps that acted as a starting point.

Sometimes this starting point is the first time you've heard of money alchemy, other times, it's that act of getting back on the bus. My clients hear me banging on about the foundations a lot, because they are so important.

When you find that your relationship with money is sliding back into negativity, ask yourself if you are doing the money magic foundations. I'm certain the answer will be either 'no' or 'not really'. That's ok, you don't need to be cross with yourself or frustrated, just get back to doing them. Get back on the bus.

Each of the foundations is created to take up a tiny amount of time. After all, we live in this reality don't we, and there's lots to do. They are things that are practical, but the result is pure magic. You'll feel better, you'll feel lighter and you'll start to see proof of money being a loving and supportive being.

I recommend doing them daily. The more you do them, the more results you'll see and the faster they will come. I often get asked 'How many should I do each day?' The aim should be to do all of them each day, but even I know that can be unrealistic. So, plan to do two each day, and see what happens.

Using the money magic foundations will connect you to money fast, but you may feel resistance or procrastination. Remember you have lived with your current thoughts and beliefs about money for a long time, and your amazing mind may need you to take a small step at a time. This is the start, or the restart. Every time you do a foundation, it ripples out into your relationship with money. So, if you are ready to commit to creating something better, this is the place to start, and the place to get you back on track.

CHAPTER SUMMARY

- The money magic foundations are things you can do to switch on abundance.

- Do as many as you can each day.

- They don't take long.

- Commit to your relationship with money by doing them.

- They work fast when you open up to doing them.

- Keep coming back to them, these are the foundations for a reason.

"THERE'S HIDDEN TREASURE EVERYWHERE"

ESSENCE & ENERGY OF MONEY CARDS

19: MONEY MAGIC FOUNDATION #1 – LOOK FOR MONEY

In this chapter, I go deep into the first of the money magic foundations. Money is trying to show you that she's there all the time, but often we're completely switched off to seeing her. This foundation will change this for you.

This may sound daft, but I promise you, we simply don't look for money. For so long, the story has been 'money is scarce '' and we believe it. Therefore, we literally look for proof of that belief; that there isn't any money around us. But the truth is, money is everywhere, (if you believe it is).

This is the very first money magic foundation because you simply will not attract more money if you are tuned out from seeing it.

It's like when you chose a new car. One that you know you haven't seen before, therefore they must be really rare. Until you choose it, and then you see them everywhere. Everyone and their dog seem to have one.

I'm gonna say this again 'money is everywhere'. Looking for money is about believing it's there. When you believe it, you will see it, not the other way round.

My client Lou told me when she first started with me, 'I know there isn't any money in my house. I need it, so I know it isn't there'. As with all of my clients, I asked her to trust the process and do the work. Within an hour, she had found over £400 in cash, in her house.

Another client messaged me in a panic as she had a big bill to pay. I reminded her to look for money and she found £1200 cash in her bedside table. This one still amazes me. She told me that a couple of years ago, she and her husband took the money out in cash for something, she couldn't remember what. Over time, she just assumed it had been spent.

The really shocking part of this story is that she opened that drawer in her bedside table almost every day, and she simply hadn't seen the money in there. Until she looked for money specifically.

Our brains are wired to find proof of our beliefs. Plant a different seed of belief and your magical mind will find proof of that instead.

Here's just some of the places my clients and I have found money:

- in the street whilst out walking
- in old bank accounts
- in our wallet/purse
- in coat pockets
- in drawers at home and at work
- in the car
- in the sofa
- in bags that haven't been used for a while
- in utility accounts — they often hold money that is actually yours
- being gifted money

Money doesn't always look like money. Remember how it alchemises into other things?

There are lots of other ways you can find money:

- returning purchases you don't love, straight away
- checking your rewards accounts such as air miles and supermarket points
- being gifted something you were thinking of buying
- getting a gift voucher
- even discounts

Can you think of other places that you could find money? The list really can be endless.

Now, you may be thinking, 'Yes that's great Eloise, but I want big bucks'. This is a foundation and that means it's the starting point, and also a key part of money work. If you do this each day, you will change your beliefs. Even if you just find a penny, it's proof that money is there and that you just need to look for it. Once you are tuned in to looking for it, you'll start to see more and more.

Now, the thing with habits like this and the other money magic foundations I'm going to share with you, is that we are often not that good at doing the things we know are good for us.

This goes for me too. I know all of the foundations work, and I get into a really good groove with them, but after a while forget about them, even though they work.

The key here is to just notice this and start again. Make a game of it. Feel joy and excitement at what you might find. Some of my most cherished finds haven't actually been money, although I do love it when I find some. Because I've been looking, with an open heart, I've found some beautiful things from nature that I still have today... feathers, pine cones, a giant conker. Also, because I was looking, I discovered so much already around me that I just hadn't seen before, like a pathway in a park that led to a quiet stream, or a nest of newly hatched cygnets (baby swans).

This habit is not just about finding money, it's about connecting with joy. And the more you do it, the more money you'll find, but the joy you'll find is worth even more.

CHAPTER SUMMARY

- Money is all around you.
- Often you just can't see it... yet.
- This foundation switches on your ability to see abundance.
- You might be surprised by just how much you haven't yet seen.

"PAYING ATTENTION TO MY MONEY HELPS ME CREATE MORE"

ESSENCE & ENERGY OF MONEY CARDS

20: MONEY MAGIC FOUNDATION #2 — MONEY LOVES ATTENTION

In this chapter, I take an in depth look at the second money magic foundation. Once you start looking for money, you might see it, but not actually pay attention to it. The idea of paying attention to money can feel overwhelming before you do it, but it's very empowering.

After money magic foundation#1 You might think your attention is on money. I did too when I first started, but there is a subtle difference between looking for money and paying attention to money. For example — have you ever seen a coin on the floor and walked past it? You saw it, but didn't pay attention.

Remember, when you work with money as a feminine being, she is just like you. She doesn't just want to be seen, she wants a little bit of attention, a bit of acknowledgement. It's the difference between 'Oh yes, you look alright' and 'oh wow — stunning — I see you!'.

Paying attention is really seeing money, and not dismissing it once you have seen it. When you see a penny in the street, pick it up and do a little happy dance or hug it — I know that sounds silly, but notice how it feels so joyful. Often when people say 'Oh it's only a penny' this translates as 'not worth paying attention to'. Imagine someone saying that about you — ouch, right? (More on this in foundation #4).

I take these smaller finds as signs from money that she's there — like when you find a white feather, you know it's a sign your Angels are around. How much time do you actually spend with money, paying her attention?

I never used to spend time with my money. I'd actually hide from it by never checking my accounts. I used to cross my fingers that my card wouldn't be declined and breathe a huge sigh of relief when the payment went through. I wasn't just not paying attention — I was actively avoiding money. No wonder she didn't want to be with me. Being avoided and ignored in a relationship does not make you feel like showing up does it? Money and you are in a relationship. Looking after that relationship is the fast track to more money.

Now my relationship with money is not avoidant or toxic. Now it's healthy, fun, supportive and playful. I check my bank accounts each day (I had to work up to this. Although it was quite scary it was always empowering). I have 'dates' with money each week, just to write finances down and plan. I dream about money consciously, and this creates happiness and expands my belief in money even more. I make sure I pay attention to, and value all money.

Many of my clients come to me with part time jobs whilst running their businesses. They are so focused on their business income that they often forget to even acknowledge their income from their job. They see it as money they don't like needing, so they dismiss it, 'It doesn't count'. (Ouch again, right?)

When I was ramping up to my first £10k month, I realised I'd been doing the same. One part of my business was making more money at the time, but because it wasn't the bit I was focussed on I completely ignored the money coming in from it. When I realised, I sat down and did the maths, and I'd been making £10k for months! So, I'd been pushing hard to get something I'd already got.

I often think the Universe must be so confused by our requests and intentions. There was me continually putting out '£10k months, £10k months'. The Universe probably just wanted to grab me and shake me and say 'I'm sending it to you!' This thought often makes me chuckle.

But it's a really powerful lesson — the Universe works on the basis of 'ask and it's given'. Just because it doesn't show up in the way you thought it would, does not mean it hasn't been given.

So, pay attention. I was stressed out that I wasn't making headway with my monthly goal. As soon as I saw it had happened and had been happening for a while, I released a lot of negativity and making more money became even easier. She wants to be seen, really seen and a bit of attention goes a long way, just like with you.

CHAPTER SUMMARY

- Often, we might see money but not actually pay attention to it.
- Money loves to spend time with you.
- You might even find you already have what you are asking for.

"DISCARDING HONES ONE'S DECISION-MAKING SKILLS."

MARIE KONDO

21: MONEY MAGIC FOUNDATION #3 – MAKE SPACE FOR MONEY

In this chapter, I go through the third foundation. I struggled for a while to see how this was relevant, but I quickly realised there are physical and symbolic things we can do to create space for money, where there currently isn't any.

When I started out on this journey, I was taught to make space for money in the form of decluttering. It felt a bit weird; how could tidying up attract money? The more I did declutter my physical environment, the more money seemed to flow to me and with growing ease. What was causing it?

Having a space that makes you feel good, even if that's just a drawer that is decluttered and tidy, adds a spring to your step. It raises your vibration to one of happiness and even joy. It feels good to have a well-ordered space. Even if you're not a tidy person, try this in just one small area. It works wonderfully.

Shortly after I figured this out, I realised there were more spaces I could declutter...

First there is your physical space; this is about the space that surrounds you every day and how you feel about it. This could be your home, your office, your car, your room. Anywhere that is physical.

Then we have headspace. How much space do we have in our head for money? Many of us don't spend much time thinking about money and so we don't have that much capacity. Others have a lot of clutter in their headspace, in the form of worry.

The third type is the heart space for money. To see and welcome money in, as a feminine, supportive and playful being, you need to have an open heart for this relationship to work beautifully.

The fourth type of space for money is energetic space. This is your field of energy which connects to money and the Universe. Often, our energetic space for money is very small because we have so many blocks, beliefs and stories about it that make it feel icky. You may even have pushed it away, so opening up your energetic space to money is really important.

So how do you make space for money in each of these spaces?

Let's start with physical space. You may have read Marie Kondo's book, *The Life-Changing Magic of Tidying, A Simple, Effective Way to Banish Clutter Forever.* This book shows you how to approach decluttering your physical space in a joyful way. Joyful as you do it, and for a long time afterwards too. To this day, I still use the principles I learned from this book. Interestingly, when my space becomes more cluttered, my money flow slows down. When I look around, I can see that I'm preventing it. So, I get back to decluttering even if that's simply emptying the bin in my office

When you have a beautiful environment, just the fact that it's tidy makes you feel better. You feel different and your vibration is higher.

When people come to me and they are starting out on their journey, what I recommend is to start the process of decluttering. The key here is not to overthink and not to overdo. Often , we can overwhelm ourselves by just thinking about decluttering, and imagining that it's going to take us a whole week/month/year. All we need to do is one small thing a day, and that might look like tidying your desk. It might look like emptying your bin (my 'go to' declutter move). It might look like tidying your clothes and decluttering those that you haven't worn before. It might look like tidying your cupboards or a drawer. It could even look like organising your purse or wallet.

What is the relevance of decluttering when it comes to money? Well, it's more to do with a universal rule, that a void will be filled. Have you ever tidied a drawer in your kitchen and before you know it, it's completely full again? Have you cleared a shelf in your office and then you realise that the whole shelf is just overflowing again?

The Universe loves to fill voids, and that's what you're creating when it comes to decluttering. You are creating a void that attracts abundance, something new.

Now let me be clear. I am not recommending you empty and declutter your bank accounts. What I'm recommending is taking your time to declutter your physical space, bit by bit. When you empty your bin, you are creating more space for more stuff.

I've mentioned the bin a few times, here's my 'bin story' that keeps repeating for me:

Emptying my bin is something I do when I notice my sales are slowing down. There may not seem to be a link, but I sell physical products as well as programs. I have a beautiful set of cards and an amazingly luxurious cheque book that my clients adore (check out the Resources sections for links to these). When I post these out it creates rubbish, comprising the usual office paraphernalia, which I put in my bin. When my bin is full it seems to be like a signal or a symbol to the Universe, that there is no space for any more orders to come in, because there's no room in my bin.

When I empty my bin, I will get an order for some cards or a cheque book within a few hours, sometimes much more instantly than that. So, emptying my bin creates space for sales, in a weird and wonderful way. Plus, the act of emptying my bin strangely feels like a nice little achievement and so my vibration rises.

Another thing I do to make space for money, is to get my address labels out and lay them on the desk. When I have these out the sales roll in, because I'm creating a void or space on those blank labels for addresses that I am going to send packages to. It took me ages to see the link and it makes me giggle because it seems so random, but it really does work.

Some other ways to create space in your business, for example, is to create files, either hard copy files or computer files for the clients that you want to attract. You don't need to know their names; you just need to create a space for those clients to come into.

Now, let's move onto the next type of space which is headspace. How much time do you spend thinking about money (positively) and dreaming about money?

One of the ways to create more space for money is to spend *time* with money, and the only way that I know that has worked for me is to put this into my diary. This is as important to me as a hospital appointment. I have to make it. I cannot cancel it. I might be able to move it, but only if that's absolutely the only option. Remember these foundations are about committing to your relationship with money. This is my money date.

I spend time dating my money, paying attention to her, looking for her, and speaking kindly to her. I also spend time dreaming about what we are going to do together in our relationship. Are we going to generate more income this month? Are we going to attract new clients? Are we going to create a new project? Are we just going to spend time together?

I use this time to check my bank accounts and to look for any other money that's coming in that, perhaps, I haven't seen. I work out what's going out and how to manifest the money for that, if it's not already there. I use it to think about the future and the present and to make plans for both.

The next space is the heart space for money. Money as a feminine being, projects a feeling of love. Now, that might take some time to sink in. We are not taught to feel love when it comes to money. We are taught the opposite, that actually, it's vulgar to talk about money. That the love of money is 'the root of all evil'. That just is not the case. When you connect with money as a feminine being, you will feel something that is familiar. It feels like love and so it's important to open your heart space to money.

One way of doing that is the visualisation in Chapter 24. You could also write a love letter to money, reflecting on your past relationship and how you want your future relationship to be.

Opening your heart space to money accelerates the relationship. It accelerates the flow of abundance, and it magnifies the feeling of ease and trust, when it comes to money, even if you aren't quite there yet. When it comes to feeling love for money, just feeling it for a fleeting moment, will have a profound and lasting impact on you.

The fourth space that you can make for money, is within your energetic space. Your energetic space for money is governed by your comfort zone. Your comfort zone is there to keep you safe. This has been programmed by your past, not your present and not your future. This means that anything that has not been experienced before is scary. Therefore, you will feel some resistance to expanding this space.

I work with my clients to expand their energetic money space, by getting them to think of the number that they are trying to manifest. I ask them to write the number down and look at it; and then I ask them to sit and hear, feel and see, all of the self-talk that's going on around that number; and often it ain't pretty. When I do this exercise, more often than not, my self-talk is laughing in the corner at me. It sucks!

We don't stop there long though. I then ask my client to double the number and write it down. Again, they sit and look at the number and become aware of even louder self-talk. Sometimes it's just completely dismissive, sometimes they can't even look at the number, let alone think about it. We sit there for a few moments paying attention to our comfort zone and energetic space, while observing that new, doubled number.

After a short while, we cross out the doubled number and look again at the first number that was written down. Invariably, the self-talk has changed from being negative and 'it's impossible', to being possible and maybe even probable. That's the sign that you have stretched your energetic space for money.

I think an energetic space for money is like a pair of tights or panty-hose. They come in a box and when you take them out, they are tiny. They probably wouldn't even fit on your foot if they weren't stretchy but when you put them on, they fit. When you take them off again though, they never return to the size they were in the box. This is how your energetic space for money works, and so carrying out that activity where you double your number, creates that stretch. When you take it off and go back to the original goal, there's less tension and less resistance from your comfort zone. Give it a go.

I've given you lots of ideas here, but a great place to start is on an actual space for money. Your purse or wallet.

I don't know about you but my purse often gets quite untidy. I even find crumbs in my purse, which always baffles me. My purse can sometimes contain crumpled up receipts, crystals and herbs, before we even get to the money and cards.

I'd like you to look at your purse or your wallet and ask yourself 'Would money like to live here?' Now this is not necessarily a physical place for money, so think of it as symbolic, especially if you don't use cash that much.

If you were money, a classy goddess like money, would you want to come and stay in your purse or wallet?

If not, you can do several things: you can give it a wipe to clean it up, you can organise your cards, you can remove your receipts and put them somewhere that they won't get lost, you can clean out the crumbs, you can refresh the herbs (if you're like me) and just make it a 5-star Air BnB instead of a one-star hostel.

When you create space for money in these four ways, it's just easier for the Universe to send it to you. It's more tempting for money to want to come and be with you, and you will find that your capacity for holding money becomes a little larger, the more you do this.

CHAPTER SUMMARY

- There are four spaces which you can declutter and expand for more money.
- The Universe loves to fill a void.
- Money is a gorgeous feminine being, treat her as you'd love to be treated.
- Invite money in by preparing for her, like an honoured guest.

"I LOVE MONEY AND MONEY LOVES ME"

ESSENCE & ENERGY OF MONEY CARDS

22: MONEY MAGIC FOUNDATION #4 – SPEAK KINDLY OF MONEY

In this chapter, I'm looking at what is arguably one of the biggest aha moments you'll have in this work. How you talk and think about money impacts how much flows to you, and how easily.

Imagine this: you're just going about your business when you hear voices chattering just around the corner. When you tune into those voices you recognise them as people who you consider to be friends. They are saying some pretty mean things about you. It's confusing and hurtful! They always ask you to lunch, and say they like and want to spend time with you, but what they are saying to each other behind your back is something different.

You move away from them, feeling pretty yucky. You even start to avoid them for a while, or maybe longer, because it hurts you to hear them say those things. You thought they liked you. Why are they saying these horrible things about you?

Now think about money as a feminine being. She's just like you. Are you behaving like those so called friends, when it comes to money? Are you saying you want money in your life, but then bitching and snitching about her?

You might think not, but let's take a closer look. Are you asking, wanting and even desiring money to come to you? If so, are you also saying or thinking things like 'money is the root of all evil', or 'money makes you mean', or 'money is hard work', or 'money is scarce?' or even 'I wish I didn't need money' and 'I hate money'. It's very likely you are. Most of us do because that's what we've been taught to do, think and feel about money.

I wonder how money feels overhearing this? Would she want to come and spend more time with you or would she be feeling disrespected, misunderstood, hurt, and confused? When you say or think negative things about money you're actually pushing her away. Thinking about money as a feminine being creates a person, and we regard people differently to energy or inanimate objects such as coins and notes.

Money is always listening, so make sure you are saying things that won't turn her away. Catch your negative thoughts or sayings and ask yourself 'What could I say instead?'

I had a really gnarly, negative thought and speech pattern about money when it came to my neighbour. Every six months or so, he'd get a new car, and I mean fancy cars too. I felt so triggered by this. I hated how he was flashing his cash as it was vulgar. I caught myself thinking this one day as I stood in my bedroom watching yet another fancy pants car come up the drive. 'Flashing cash is vulgar.'' OMG! I don't even know where that came from. I pictured money being told she was vulgar and imagined how I'd feel if someone ever said this to me. Ouch! That was tough.

I decided there and then to start thinking differently. It wasn't easy and I still felt triggered every six months. Instead, I chose to think 'That's his expression of his connection with money. That's wonderful'. Over time, this got easier and I actually started to look out for the next car. This came from my own junk around money. I'm not that fussed about cars. At the time of writing this, I drive a little Toyota Aygo. I don't really understand why people like cars so much, but I get that some do. And that's ok. Money is always listening — be kind!

CHAPTER SUMMARY

- Money is always listening.

- Speaking unkindly of money pushes it away.

- Catch your negative thoughts and words and ask yourself 'What could I think/say instead?'

"I AM FILLED WITH GRATITUDE FOR MONEY"

ESSENCE & ENERGY OF MONEY CARDS

23: MONEY MAGIC FOUNDATION #5 – MONEY LOVES TO BE APPRECIATED

> In this chapter, I explore the fifth foundation. Just like you, money loves to be appreciated and here are some ways you can show your appreciation for it.

This foundation is about gratitude. We all like a bit of gratitude for what we do, don't we? Well, so does money.

The truth is money has been there for you most of your life. It may have felt hard at times, but even when I was at my worst, having my home repossessed, I still had money. Nowhere near as much as I needed, or wanted, but it was still there.

Somehow, with no credit rating I managed to put a roof over mine and my son's head, and we never went hungry. There was even a time, when I couldn't provide for myself, and I managed to qualify for benefits — this is money too. Even though it can have a very heavy feeling linked to it, this is money supporting you.

Showing gratitude for money is a beautiful thing. It raises your feelings of love and joy and shows money that you appreciate her.

Think about a time someone was grateful to you. It leaves you with a lovely spring in your step, and you feel really connected to that person, don't you? Doing more with them feels perfect. Money is the same.

Gratitude is a practice that I have found raises my vibration and my feelings in general, and since I've been doing it I've been happier across my life. When it's easy, it's really easy. I just list all of the wonderful ways money has been there for me on that day....

Some of the wonderful ways money has been there for me:

- sales
- royalties
- refunds
- finding £1
- my friend buying lunch
- being gifted something
- finding a savings account I'd forgotten about etc

When it's hard though, it can feel impossible. On those days when I'm not feeling the money vibe at all I start small. Slowly it starts to get easier and easier.

The key is to keep at it, especially when it's hard and you don't want to, as that is the time you need it the most.

Here's how my list starts on the bad days:

- money makes sure I have clean water to drink
- I am warm in my bed thanks to the duvet that money got me
- I had money to nourish my body and mind today

I used to feel really guilty when I didn't feel grateful for money, but sometimes it's just hard to feel it. Don't beat yourself up.

Money is so forgiving and kind, even a little tiny bit of effort will be rewarded. I send appreciation to money each day before I go to sleep. I think of three things, although often it's many more, and thank money for them. There are some other ways that you can show appreciation to money too.

Here are just some that my clients and I use.

1. HAPPY DANCES

Think of these as mini celebrations, when you find money, make a sale, or money just comes to you in any of its forms. Do a little dance, whoop, sing, cheer, whatever, but celebrate. Even if it's just a penny in the street, celebrate money. It may feel silly at first, but I love doing it now. If you forget to celebrate just do it when you remember.

2. ABUNDANCE BOWL

This is a gorgeous way to centre your attention and appreciation each day. Find a nice bowl, but don't overthink this, any bowl will do for now.

Make a commitment to add something to the bowl every day, or every week. Whatever feels right for you. Then, every time you find money, feathers, conkers, leaves you like the look of or anything that reminds you of how abundant the world is, place it in your bowl. This lovely practice connects you to the world and money in such a wonderful way.

Every time you feel the desire, empty your bowl and look through all the lovely things you've collected. Appreciate each one and be reminded that abundance that is all around.

3. MONEY CORNER / ALTAR

This is my favourite way to show appreciation for money. I have a money altar. It's just a corner in my house that I have dedicated to the gorgeous feminine being we call money. My abundance bowl sits on it and when I empty my bowl, I rearrange all of the money things and switch it all around.

You can make it as obvious or subtle as you want. You might want to have things that simply represent money, or money itself there. Or a mix of both.

On my money altar, I have:

- two green candles (green is the colour of money and prosperity)
- a money affirmation card (see the resources page for details)
- herbs such as basil and rosemary sprinkled around
- nutmegs and cloves to bring luck
- ribbons
- crystals (see chapter on crystals)
- a statue of Goddess Fortuna
- a £10 note with a post-it on it, thanking money for all that she's brought to me

Your corner or altar may look very different to mine, as this is a really personal thing. Start small, with one or two things, and use it to draw your focus back to money every time you tend to it, or reorganise it.

Add as much, or as little as you want, and use only things you are drawn to.

Your corner or altar will evolve over time, as your relationship with money evolves, and so it is very personal and precious to you.

CHAPTER SUMMARY

- Money is like you — a bit of appreciation goes a long way.
- Gratitude for money can feel hard sometimes — start small.
- Make a list of the ways money was there for you today.
- Create an altar or corner for your money so you can appreciate it visually.

PART III
MONEY MUSINGS

So far in this book, I've covered some key concepts and approaches to money. In this part of the book, I want to give you some practical things and stories you can use, to connect with money and develop your relationship with her. These work in conjunction with the money magic foundations, which underpin all of the money alchemy work.

When you step into healing and transforming your relationship with money, you open up the flow of abundance, and more than that, you will notice how wonderful it feels.

There is a beautiful side effect of this work, which I've mentioned a few times. When you do this work you will start to like, and even love yourself.

Take what works, leave what doesn't, adapt it to work for you. These are not prescriptions, just guidance based on my own research and experience. Don't feel like you should be doing all of them? Pick one or two to try and give them a go, add in your own elements as your confidence grows.

Remember this is a practice, a journey and repetition is often your friend. As with alchemy generally, money alchemy is about tweaking, to fine tune your transformations.

"WHEN I BELIEVE IN ABUNDANCE, I WILL SEE IT."

ESSENCE & ENERGY OF MONEY CARDS

24: YOUR OWN PERSONAL MONEY GODDESS

In this chapter, I'm going to take you on a journey to actually meet money. Yes, you read that correctly. This will help you connect with her as a feminine being, and see her in a completely new light.

I've recorded this for you so you can experience it fully, but if you'd like to read along, that's fine too. You'll find the recording on the resources page at the end of this book.

As you prepare to journey with me, to meet your gorgeous money Goddess, make sure you are somewhere quiet, warm and comfortable. Don't use it whilst driving or operating machinery — you know the drill lovely!

This guided visualisation will show you money in a completely different way. You'll be surprised for sure! You'll also notice that it has a really calming effect to see money in this way. So spend a few moments, preferably several minutes enjoying that feeling afterwards.

Don't overthink this, just enjoy what comes. If you struggle to visualise, imagine or day dream instead. Whatever you see or don't see is fine for you.

Some of my clients actually fall asleep as they listen to this, and whilst that's a wonderful thing, to drift off with money, if it happens to you, it can be a sign of resistance. Don't give up, after a few tries, you'll be able to listen to it all and enjoy the full magic within it.

Meet money visualisation:

- Sit with your feet on the ground and take some deep breaths.
- Imagine you can breathe right into your hips, full and deep breaths.
- When you are ready, close your eyes.
- Feel your feet on the floor and become aware of their connection.
- Imagine you can see roots, like tree roots, growing from them and embed them into the ground.
- You see, money is 'of this earth', so connecting with money is grounding as well as inspiring.
- Imagine these roots growing deep into the core of the earth, keeping you connected.
- Slowly, coming into your awareness, you sense something.
- Something warm.
- Something intriguing.
- Something wonderful.
- And you become aware that you can see money.
- She might be a person, or a stack of cash, or some gorgeous energy.
- Spend time noticing her, the colours, the fabrics or textures.
- Now imagine you can hear money. What does she sound like?
- Is she singing, rustling or chinking like coins, or maybe she is silent.
- What scent are you noticing? Flowers, perfume, paper, metal, nothing. Just notice.
- And now become aware of the movement of money as she stands before you.
- Is she calm and still, swishing and swirling, floating and flowing?
- She may not be how you thought she'd be.

- She'll appear to you just as you need her to right now.
- She always knows.
- Imagine you can see her, or sense her beckoning to you.
- She wants to tell you something.
- She wants to share something and maybe even give you something.
- Move towards her and sit with her for a few minutes, enjoying the feeling and receiving what she is saying and giving.
- After a while, thank her and hold that wonderful feeling of gratitude for a few moments.
- Allow her image, scent, sound and feeling to fade until you become aware of your feet and those roots connecting you to the Earth.
- Have a little stretch and when you are ready take a deep breath and open your eyes.

Notice how you feel and jot down your thoughts and experiences.

What was it like to meet money and how did she differ from all the things you thought and felt about her?

This visualisation is one of my favourite things to do (I have a lot of these). It's very often the first time you've ever felt something other than worry, when it comes to money. Use it whenever you feel disconnected from money, or just want to feel the beautiful energy that surrounds her.

It feels like a very special secret knowing her in this way. I treasure every journey to meet her and in my monthly membership, Money Alchemy Circle, we work with money in this way each month. She is wise and kind, as you have no doubt experienced.

CHAPTER SUMMARY

- This journey to meet money will transform how you feel about her.
- Money is wise and kind as a feminine being.
- You can use this visualisation to meet her any time.

"MY RELATIONSHIP WITH MONEY REFLECTS MY RELATIONSHIP WITH MYSELF."

ESSENCE & ENERGY OF MONEY CARDS

25: THE MONEY MIRROR

In this chapter, I'll show you your very own *money mirror*. It can take time for the penny to drop (pun intended) but when it does, you'll see that you can work either with money or yourself and the other will benefit too.

You'll often hear me say: 'Your relationship with money is a direct reflection of your relationship with yourself.'

People often look very confused when they hear me say this for the first time. Like it just doesn't make any sense. But after working with me for a while or simply just being in my world, they often message with 'OMG, I get it now'.

As women, we often have a priority list. More often than not you are not on your own list.

What this looks like is:
- putting yourself last, if anywhere at all
- spending money on everyone but yourself
- feeling guilty about spending money on yourself
- neglecting your needs and wants
- losing yourself and no longer even knowing what you want

- lack of dreams about the future
- a feeling of 'is this all there is?' coupled with guilt around having lots of great stuff in your life
- (my favourite) — underwear or clothes with holes in them — yes, I know this may seem daft but seriously, look at your underwear and it will show you your relationship with yourself

If you feel any of these things, your relationship with yourself needs and deserves more focus. Also, I'm willing to bet that if you feel any of these, then your relationship with money is just as neglectful.

The word 'perfunctory' comes to mind here:

"carried out without real interest, feeling, or effort."

Oxford Languages

How awful is that? Most of us go through life without putting any thought into ourselves or money? Are you paying any attention to yourself or money? If so, is it positive and kind? Or negative and neglectful?

When I first started out on this journey, I couldn't even say that I liked myself. Now I'm starting to feel like I actually love who I am, and how I am. Working on my relationship with money has done this. I realised a few years ago that despite everything we are told about money, it actually is love. The vibration of money is high, like love, angels and your higher self.

When you really listen to money, she only speaks with love and kindness to you. Everything else is likely to be conditioning or your ego. Therefore, when you start working on that relationship with money, you feel totally supported and loved. You have fun and feel resourceful. What happens when you feel like this? You feel happier, you are kinder to yourself and more confident in who you are.

Money may not be able to buy happiness, but it is a route to finding it within yourself. When you develop a deep connection that you trust with money your flow of abundance opens up, not just to money, but to love, joy, happiness… everything.

Society teaches us that money is the root of all evil etc., but when you work with money as a feminine being she becomes the path back to love.

You can do this the other way around too. You can work on loving yourself and then the money will flow more easily — because money is a mirror. But, if you're anything like me when I started out, the thought of even liking myself felt like a stretch; so, money was a gorgeous energy to work with as I developed this acceptance, like, appreciation and then love of myself.

The money mirror can also show you patterns in other parts of your life too: food, health, relationships, friendships, work progression etc. It will help you to identify blocks, stories, beliefs and patterns that have transferred from one part of your life to another so that you can release them.

Hold up that mirror — look at how you treat yourself. What similarities are there to how you treat money and vice versa?

Now that you know about the money mirror, what can you do? Treat this like a new relationship. Start slow, get to know money and yourself, and allow yourself to be loved and abundant. A great place to start are the money magic foundations as these can form part of your everyday life.

Having a fabulous relationship with yourself is the side effect of working with money alchemy. I'll be honest, I wasn't expecting that, but I see it in myself and all of my clients. When you feel great about yourself, it's like the sun comes out. Even when things are hard, you know, for a fact: you've got this.

Remember, this works both ways: Work on your relationship with money, and your relationship with yourself will improve. Work on your relationship with yourself, and your relationship with money will improve.

So here are a few suggestions to help you get started on both:

Relationship with money	Relationship with self
Money magic foundations.	Take a bath (if you like them).
Check your accounts.	Have a nap.
Create a money space or altar.	Read for fun.
Say nice things about money (inside and outside your head).	Say nice things about yourself (inside and outside your head).
Welcome money into your life, regardless of whether you earned it.	Book a lunch break in your diary every day for you do things for you.
Release money blocks and shame so you can invite more money in.	Eat something that nourishes your body.
Notice when you get scared and voice it.	Let go of perfectionism — you are already good enough.

I know this can seem odd, or even scary, but try it. Just like everything I talk about, you will see results fast, if you do the work!

CHAPTER SUMMARY

- Money is a mirror to your relationship with yourself.
- This can be hard to see at first.
- Being kind to money makes you kinder to yourself, and vice versa.
- There are lots of ways to work on this and change the reflection that you see.

"MONEY IS ALL AROUND ME."

ESSENCE & ENERGY OF MONEY CARDS

26: MONEY IS EVERYWHERE

In this chapter, I'm going to challenge scarcity with you. You might be looking at the title and thinking 'no way', so let's change that. When you start to see money everywhere, it'll make you giggle for sure.

'Money is everywhere' can be really hard to believe when you have had a lifetime of scarcity and struggle, but I promise that there is money very close to you right now.

I get it. You're sitting there thinking, or maybe even yelling, 'Of course there isn't Eloise, if there was, I'd know about it'.

I spent some of my teen years in extreme poverty, scabbling around to find 50 pence for the electric metre. Money was hard and extremely scarce. It was the same for everyone on the estate. It was a really miserable time in my life, and when I think about it, my memories are all grey and rainy. That doesn't mean we didn't have good times. I certainly laughed a lot during this time, but life was just very hard.

This was a pattern I repeated right into my late 30s. Even when I had more money, it would disappear. I was caught up in a pattern of scarcity and I had no idea how to change that, because it was all I had ever known.

My debt just grew and grew and with it the shame of my debt. My shame of the bad decisions I'd made. I hated money. I hated that I needed money. Money was really hard. But what if I told you it doesn't have to be that way anymore? Seeing money everywhere needs a shift in your perspective, and it's one of my favourite things to do.

From an early age, it's likely that you will have heard a lot of things about money. That it's scarce, that it's the root of all evil, that it makes sure the rich get richer and the poor get poorer, and more. As a result of these messages about money, you actually stop seeing it. When you start seeing money everywhere it's like having a new pair of glasses. Everything is clearer and more vibrant.

The really fantastic thing is that you are still experiencing the same life. It's just there is more abundance, and abundance makes joy and happiness so much easier. Is it going to stop bad things happening? No, I'm afraid not — that's life. But this new view, on money specifically and on abundance generally, will make it easier to navigate the tougher times too.

As I sit in my office writing this, I'm reminded of how everything in it, was created somehow with money. I also know that if I go and look for money I will find it, one way or another.

Here are just some of the things I can see in my office that money provided:
- crystals
- computer
- phone
- ring light
- notebook and pen
- desk
- paint on walls
- carpet
- windows
- seat
- bowl of money
- incense sticks
- mug of tea

All of these items on the list were achieved just by spending a moment thinking about how money is all around me. The list is endless.

If you have things, the chances are money got them for you. Even if you were given them, money was used to obtain these things.

Money has supported me (and you) much more than we think it has, throughout our lives. Even though we are convinced it's scarce and hard and yucky, it's been there for you. Imagine what would change if you had the belief that money is, in fact, everywhere. Not only that, but also that it can come to you from all sorts of places, not just your job or business. Often people fail to even see money that they haven't earned. Like it doesn't count. This leads to a very limited focus on money.

When I first started manifesting the money for my home, I was so caught up in what I earned, I simply could not see how we were ever going to be able to save anything. Let alone enough to buy the house we dreamed of.

I would do the sums with our salaries and it just didn't add up to enough. I thought it would take at least ten years to save the money for the deposit. Just nine months later we were in. We even had enough money to fully furnish and decorate the house, and even go on holiday to Italy for a week. Where had all the money come from?

Everywhere.

Once I started applying the principles in this book, it was like money was raining on us. It came from expected places, and completely out of the blue places. I even started looking for money, not really expecting much, but finding huge amounts.

There were bonuses, refunds, gifts, freebies. And, whilst none of these were huge, it just seemed to welcome even more in. I got home one day to a cheque for £11,555. This was a PPI reclaim I'd made on the off chance. Two weeks later, another one for £9,000 landed. I didn't even think I'd get a penny, and so for many years I hadn't bothered, thinking 'there's no money for me'. What other money had I let slip through my fingers?

I'd been ignoring money and thinking 'It's not for me'. As soon as I started working on my desire to manifest a home, money came.

What you focus on becomes real. I'd been focusing on scarcity and lack, all my life, and guess what I got? Yep, scarcity and lack. In just nine short months of focusing on money and abundance, that's what I got — money and abundance.

So, when I say 'money is everywhere', I know this to be true. I also know that if I say 'money is hard' — that will become true. I choose the first one now. It's not always easy with society, the media, friends and family, who still choose the latter. I get moments of doubt, especially when the tough stuff happens. That's when I sit and list all the things money has brought to me, one way or another.

In my darkest days with money, it was still there for me. It was almost impossible to see, but it was there. I see that now. So, if you're ready to choose 'money is everywhere', you're in the right place.

One of the biggest things to let go of when it comes to money is worry. We have made worrying a bit of a pastime, and it really does hinder every part of our life. There's a proverb about money which I think sums it up very well:

'Worrying about money is like a rocking chair. It gives you something to do but doesn't get you anywhere.'

Worrying creates awful feelings and has the added non-bonus of making time drag, so you get to experience worry for even longer. Worrying about anything, especially money, has never made any positive difference to anyone. It keeps you busy doing nothing, except feeling bad. But what can you do instead?

Anything else! I know that's actually very easy to say when you are worrying, but literally anything else will help. Every single page in this book contains things to think about and do instead. When you shift out of worry, even if it's just for a moment, you will feel lighter. The magic of manifesting is not about the figure, it's about the feeling. Shifting that feeling into something good, like the feeling that money is everywhere and spending time seeing it will make you feel better.

Better feelings equal a better connection to yourself and to money. And that's attractive.

Open your mind to attracting money, from everywhere and anywhere, and you will become attractive to money. Spend time worrying, and you'll attract more worry.

Of course, worry is intrusive. You can be minding your own business and then it hits you. At this point recognise it and do something else, something from this book. Then repeat when the worry kicks in again. Worrying about money is probably something you've been doing for a big part of your life, so it will take some time to let it go.

Now, I'm not saying you should be reckless and not bother to think about what you need to pay. I'm saying that there are many ways to interact with money that feel good, rather than heavy. Remember, it's the feeling we want — the good feeling.

Open up to money being everywhere and coming to you from all directions... some you can't even imagine right now.

CHAPTER SUMMARY

- Money is everywhere and anywhere.
- Scarcity takes away our belief in this concept.
- Worrying closes it off too.
- Open up to money coming from all directions and it will appear.

"THE MORE I HAVE,
THE MORE PEOPLE I CAN HELP."

ESSENCE & ENERGY OF MONEY CARDS

27: WHY ENOUGH IS NEVER ENOUGH

> In this chapter, I go into some depth on why asking for 'just enough' is actually keeping you in scarcity and limiting your ability to manifest abundance.

'I just want enough to... ' is one of the most common things I hear from my clients. They say it because they want more but don't want to feel greedy.

Greedy is a word that brings shame. To be accused of it or be seen as greedy, simply feels awful. Greed is an unknown limit which caps your ability to be abundant. Greed is a judgement by others and by yourself, but it is just a story because you are meant to be abundant. Abundance is never ending. 'Enough' has an end point and by asking for enough, you're asking to be stuck in the struggle.

What "enough" will get you:
- Having enough to go on holiday once a year will ensure you have enough for that, but not for the emergencies that crop up, such as when your car needs fixing.
- Having enough to pay for your child's wedding, will get you enough to do this but you'll find buying your own dress for this wedding feels hard.

- Having enough really means a shift in priorities whilst keeping your wants and needs off your own agenda.
- 'Enough' is enough — and no more. There's no allowance for excess, for emergencies or other priorities. There's 'just enough'.

This creates a ceiling or limit on what you are going to bring into your life. So, what should you be asking for instead? More than enough. Or even better...

An abundance. Abundance is infinite, it cannot be limited.

But how do you get away from that shameful feeling of being greedy by wanting more? I still get twinges of 'It's greedy to want or ask for more', so now I run through some questions quietly, and slowly let it go.

'Who says it's greedy?' Normally, I find this isn't even my thought. It's a thought I've taken on from someone else, or society. As we are meant to be abundant — asking for more is never greedy, it's as it should be. Also, remember that every single person has a different concept of what greed is. Think about those conversations you've had about winning the lottery. How bad does it feel to even think about keeping it all? Each of your friends will have a different amount that they feel they can keep without feeling greedy. It's a really fascinating conversation to observe.

'Am I going to do bad things with more money?' I don't recall ever thinking about doing something bad with more money. Remember that your relationship with money is a direct reflection of your relationship with yourself. It's not selfish to want to have and do things for yourself. It's filling your cup up so that it overflows. Everyone benefits from this.

'Will I get lazy with more money?' Oooooo, this 'lazy' word is shameful too isn't it. But it comes from the story we're told that to have more money you must work harder or else you don't deserve more money. What if 'lazy' actually looks like: happier, more relaxed, healthier,

aligned, recharged. It's not lazy to have money and it's not lazy to work less and generate more income. That's smart!

'Will I lose people from my life if I have more money?' This is a tough one. I have lost people from my life when I've increased my income. What I've learned is that people are often very caught in the struggle. They can't see a different way, only the struggle. When I started to move away from that, they judged me. They thought I'd changed, but all I'd done was to let go of the struggle. In some cases, this was the thing that we had in common and that had gone. After years of feeling very hurt about people moving away from my life, I realised that these people weren't on this part of the journey with me. Maybe they will be later. I used to want everyone to come along with me, to experience abundance and step out of the pain of the struggle, but the truth is familiarity is comfortable even if it's negative. Some people get trapped in who you were and struggle to see you evolve. That's their stuff, not yours. So yes, you may lose people from your life if you have more money, but those people are on their own journey, and that's ok.

'What will I do if I actually have more than enough?' Trust me, this will reveal itself to you as it happens. I used to worry that I'd be bored or even feel quite depressed (I thought this was odd when I first thought of it, but it comes back to the comfiness of struggle). What I've found is that you will become more *you*, and that fills the time beautifully, because you'll attract things to do that fill you up even more.

The funny thing about asking for more is that, for many of us, it's scary. We think failure is what we fear, but the thought of ease, success and abundance is actually far more terrifying because most of us haven't experienced it. It feels like travelling to a very unfamiliar place where you know nobody, can't speak the language and everything is different from home. The reality is, once you've spent a little time feeling it out, it feels like a wonderful, warm, peaceful and fun place.

So, aim for more than enough. Aim for abundance. Know that your fears stop you from experiencing the peace and ease that follow.

CHAPTER SUMMARY

- If you ask for 'just enough' you are not asking for abundance.
- Abundance is infinite and therefore limitless.
- Ask the questions, and add in your own when you start to limit yourself.

"THE FEELING IS MORE IMPORTANT
THAN THE FIGURE."

28: YOU ARE REPELLING MONEY

In this chapter, I explore how you might be repelling money, even though you think and feel like you are manifesting it. This can be really frustrating and you may even see money coming towards you, but not actually getting to you. It gets held up.

'I desperately need money.'

'I want more money, but it just isn't coming.'

These are things people say when they are new to the world of money alchemy.

Often, we think we are manifesting money when actually we are re-pelling it, or rather, manifesting a greater lack of money. As I mentioned before, we are always manifesting. You, for example, might be thinking you are manifesting more and struggle to understand why it's getting harder and harder.

It's about the feeling, not the figure. The feeling is the most important part of manifesting money. Your language often shows your true feelings.

'Need' is very powerful. We all have needs and it really does feel like you need money, right? But if you need money, that underlying feeling is negative and what you actually manifest is more need of money.

'Want' sounds better, doesn't it? Well, not really. Often 'want' comes from 'don't want'. 'I want the money to hire a cleaner', is actually a 'don't want': 'I don't want to do the cleaning anymore'. Although this is lighter than need it still has a negative undertone.

Pay attention to what you are thinking and saying about money. We have a lot of negativity around money, and as covered earlier, money is always listening.

If you are ignoring the money that is coming into your life, this can repel it too. So many times, in my life I've found myself feeling desperate for money, but completely ignoring the money I did have or could access. I remember, I once had to claim benefits, and I said out loud, and in my head, 'It doesn't count because I didn't earn it'.

I honestly think the Universe must get so frustrated with us.

The tricky bit about needs and wants is that they are real. You really do need and want money, but how do you manifest what you need and want without manifesting more need and want? Desire!

Desire is the key feeling needed for manifesting. So, what do you desire? Desire is something many of us have cut off from. I remember, when I first met my friend Lucienne she told me she would spend time each day dreaming.

The Universe doesn't actually see the difference between our imagined reality and our 'real' reality. It's all real. And it's all about the feeling. So, daydreaming made immediate sense to me. Desire is more than just a thought though, it's a whole body, mind and soul experience. That's why when you desire something it's so clear. You don't just see it, you feel it and become it.

Desire will likely not come easily to you after decades of not allowing it, so here's my practical approach to it: after a while, it will become easier and more natural.

The DESIRE process	
D is for Dream	Give yourself time to dream, even a few moments is enough. Close your eyes and imagine how life will be different when you have all the money you need or want. Focus on the vision of having it, rather than needing or wanting it. Be playful and don't put any pressure on yourself. If you can't see or feel anything, just imagine it.
E is for Explore	Move around in this dream. What else do you find and feel? Sometimes I notice some money blocks or stories and I jot them down for later. Other times I notice things that have a ripple effect on receiving more. Every time you come back to this desire you'll find more.
S is for Sense	Tune into your senses. What can you see, hear, feel, taste or smell? Use your imagination here and remember the Universe sees it all as real. Again, if you struggle with this, just imagine. We all receive information in different ways, so whatever you get is perfect for you.
I is for Intention	Decide here and now to draw this new vision towards you. This is an intention. It's a powerful form of goal setting. The most important difference between an intention and a goal is that with an intention you don't plan each step. You let go of 'the how' and you stop yourself thinking of 'the how' and just allow the journey to unfold.
R is for Revisit	Go back to seeing your desire again. Go through the same process and sharpen the sense you have of it. Thanks to Lucienne, I now schedule my 'desire' daydream sessions. I book them into my diary each day, but even doing this once a

	week will do the trick. Feel the feeling, magnify it and bask in it. It's the feeling that makes the difference. And remember, this is just a dream. It's perfectly safe to go big. You'll start to feel more comfortable in your desires the more often you do this. And that's when the magic really starts to happen.
E is for Expand	Add more details to it. Design your desire. This is the really fun bit. It's like a future story unfolding before your eyes. Keep spotting new details and surprise elements, and notice the feeling of desire expanding. Focussing on your desire is a far happier feeling as it moves you away from need and want, even if just for a moment. It sends a different, highly attractive and magnetic energy out to money and The Universe. Plus, it gives you a short break from the pressure. The more you do this the better you'll feel about money, and that will result in manifesting amazing things with much more ease.

Keep practising this until it becomes part of your own manifesting magic.

CHAPTER SUMMARY

- You may want or need money but this can actually repel it.
- Focus on the feeling.
- The DESIRE process will help you draw it towards you instead.

"MONEY COMES FROM MANY SOURCES AND DIRECTIONS."

ESSENCE & ENERGY OF MONEY CARDS

29: LETTING GO OF THE HOW

In this chapter, I cover the number one thing that slows down your money manifestations; the 'how'. I'll also give you some tips on how to let go of this.

Have you ever thought about something you'd like to have, create or achieve in your life, and then realised you didn't know how? Most times, this creates frustration and confusion and leads to letting that dream go. All because you can't figure out the 'how'.

The how is something that creates a known pathway before you arrive at it, and there is a lot of pressure to know the how.

When you are manifesting anything, especially money, letting go of the how is an important part of the process.

In employment, you've probably experienced several meetings during which senior leaders share their vision for the organisation, and then explain each step in a strategy. The how is the strategy, the roadmap, the steps to take. This is clear and everyone feels safe and secure knowing this.

When I first trained as a coach, there was a huge focus on goal setting and strategy. There still is. There's nothing wrong with this if you are solely focused on the practical and logical side of things. I found though, that this approach really didn't work for me. I had big goals and my first clients did too, but we just got completely stuck on the how. This led to feelings of not being ready, or not feeling qualified enough or as though the goals were just too big.

You see, when you have an emotional connection to your goal, lack of clarity can feel like failure or as if it's just too far away for you to reach.

This always brought me back to 'This is all there is?'. As I couldn't see the path clearly, I felt disheartened and stuck.

So, what should you do instead? Set your desire or intention (aka goal) and then let go of the how.

This does go against my training as a coach, but I promise you I have had so much more success since I started doing this, and my clients experience huge shifts in their manifestations too.

When you set yourself a big goal or intention, it's exciting. It's like standing at the foot of Mount Everest, looking up and thinking 'I'm gonna climb that'. Then reality kicks in — it's so high, it's much steeper than it looks, it's not an easy stroll around the park, I'm not trained for this, most people can't do it etc. The goal becomes so overwhelming, so hard that you disconnect from it, and when you disconnect from it, you stop drawing it towards you. Or you sit down to write a plan, and by realising just how much work and planning needs to go into it you lose all confidence and patience with it.

Letting go of the how means setting those goals, and then focusing only on finding the first step. Then, when you've done that you focus on finding the next step. Letting go of the how, is knowing that you don't yet know what that step is or looks like, but being open to seeing it. Some people call this 'surrendering to the Universe' which it is.

When you work with magic of any type, it is about skills, yes, but it's also about faith. Being able to trust that the Universe will show you the way at the right time, is a secret that changes everything. Knowing that what you desire is always getting drawn to you. It's done the moment you think it and feel it. Your only job is to allow it rather than prevent it. The Universe knows the best way to get things to you, and if you focus on the how you might not see it. This doesn't mean sitting on the sofa will get you your goals. It means being alert and open to opportunities, actions, different directions and signs as you arrive at them.

Goal setting is a logical process which relies on clear plans and time-lines.

Manifestation is a magical process which relies on faith, openness and a sense of humour! Honestly, I laugh almost every day at the signs and opportunities that the Universe shows me. I would never have thought of them in a million years! Manifesting money can sometimes be so fast that you can't even see the how when looking back, For example, when Mark and I manifested the money to buy our home, we had so much money come from so many directions, and some of it we still can't figure out. Sometimes it's so fast, that you don't even notice that you've got to the top of the mountain.

In June of 2022, I finally decided, after 20 years, that I was going to go ahead with having a breast reduction. I needed £10,000 to cover the operation and some time off afterwards. This was in addition to my usual monthly outgoings. I used a Magical Manifestation Cheque (see chapter 36 for more details) but got a bit stuck in the how. I caught this and just placed the cheque on my money altar and left it there, getting out of my head and out of the how.

I saw the surgeon in July and the operation was booked for the beginning of October. In the middle of September, I had a wobble, 'but how?' Again, I caught this and just started doing more of the money magic foundations each day. The following week, I found out I had money in the business. Guess how much? £10,0000! Now I pay attention to my money, but somehow, previously this had been ignored by my subconscious. I checked with my accountant who told me I would pay tax on it, but we could treat it like a bonus.

I thought I'd have a really slow month after the operation, as I wouldn't be working for three weeks. I couldn't even bring myself to check my accounts whilst I was off. That month, I had my first ever £20,000 month in my business whilst I was recovering from surgery.

'How, how, how?' I asked as I stared in disbelief at my numbers when I finally looked at them. I stopped, smiled and allowed it.

I could never have imagined money being there for me in that way. I was working on scaling my business and this means a lot of outlay. But there it was, waiting for me.

When you cast an intention it's immediately in motion, coming towards you. It may even have already manifested. All you have to do is get out of the way and follow the path, as it reveals itself to you. You don't need all of the directions. You just need to put one foot in front of the other until the next turn becomes visible.

Letting go of the how is easy for me to say, but it's not quite so easy to do, even for me. So how do you do it?

As with any part of money alchemy, simply being aware that you're hooked onto the how is powerful in itself. Once you become aware of something, it loses its power and loosens its grip on you. Once you see it you can choose to stop it and let go of it.

Now, like the money blocks, stories and beliefs, the how is a sneaky thing. You'll put it down and all of sudden, it's back. When this happens, I say 'I'm surrendering this to The Universe/Money'. Saying things out loud is also very powerful. You can say whatever works for you. In fact, many spell and prayer endings are actually words of surrender.

The word, amen, for example, simply means 'so be it'. ' It is done' and 'so mote it be' are other examples of this. They all are statements that assume that whatever it is you have requested, is already done and on its way.

Speaking is spellcasting, but so is writing; you are literally spelling your wish into being. Instead of doubting or worrying about the way, just assume it is already done and focus on looking out for it, rather than why it can't happen. It may seem daft to say things out loud but try it. I used to think I could just say it in my head, and this does work a bit, but when I speak it, when I hear it in my own voice, it adds magic and power to the words.

My favourite and most powerful way to let go of the how is to state or cast my intention, and then do something else to keep my mind and body more occupied. The money magic foundations are my go-to. Firstly, because you're so focused on looking for abundance, you'll get signs and directions even faster. But also, ramping up how much you do then creates a longer term impact, like me having my best month ever whilst I wasn't working. They keep you thinking and moving towards what you asked for, rather than worrying that you don't yet have all the directions.

CHAPTER SUMMARY

- The how gets in the way of your desire.
- Goals can be overwhelming.
- Focus on finding the next step only.
- Speak your release of 'the how'.
- Distract yourself from 'the how' with the money magic foundations.

"I AM WORTHY OF BEING WEALTHY."

ESSENCE & ENERGY OF MONEY CARDS

30: RETURN TO WORTHINESS

In this chapter, I take a look at worthiness and what creates it. Women often feel unworthy, especially when it comes to success and money, and we have plenty of reasons to back up that feeling. The truth is, you are worthy.

I don't know about you, but I have a whole list of reasons why I don't feel worthy. Worthy of love, worthy of success, worthy of happiness and especially worthy to have and hold money. These are all things I want, but because I don't feel I've been a perfect person all my life, I've struggled to feel that I even deserve worthiness.

Sometimes I think I'm worthy of something, and then my inner voice kicks in and reminds me of a time when I did something that wasn't deserving of being worthy.

Worthiness isn't something you earn. You are born worthy and remain worthy. It's a solid state. Even if you've done bad things, this doesn't mean you are a bad person. Worthiness remains. I am still working on this. I still seek some sort of confirmation, from outside of myself, that I am worthy. Worthy of love, worthy of being cared for, worthy of being wealthy, worthy of being successful. Your worthiness is inside of you, not outside. It's often beaten down by negative self-talk and experiences which you run over and over again in your mind.

I find that the best way to truly feel worthy, is to trust myself in terms of who I am and how I show up. Once you can do that, then worthiness will become easier and more natural. Being able to practise self-care, giving yourself permission to be a human being with faults and accepting your unique gifts, are all additional ways of strengthening your worthiness.

Take time to remember that you are worthy of everything you desire. You are valuable and can achieve any goals or dreams you set for yourself. As a daily practice, I imagine a gorgeous little crown in my heart. My crown of worthiness. In my mind I place it on my head. Like me, you are worthy, and worthiness is something only you can give or take away from yourself.

This may seem a bit daft, but more than anything, this tiny, momentary visualisation reminds me that 'I choose'. I choose to be worthy. I choose to allow this state and I choose to remember that it's only me that can make that choice.

Remembering this simple truth helps me stay grounded in the understanding of my own worthiness. That I am worthy of all the things I desire in life. So, take a few moments and remind yourself that you *are* worthy. You have been from the beginning, and remain so throughout your journey. Live as if you already know this to be true, and you will start to see shifts in your life where worthiness is concerned.

Believe in your worthiness and trust yourself to be the amazing, incredible human being you are. You have been worthy all along. Now, it's up to you to believe it. Here's an example to help with this...

The value of a £50 note

If I have a £50 note — how much is it worth? No, that's not a trick question — it's worth £50, right?

What if I screw it up, rip it a bit, drop it on the floor and stamp all over it? How much is it worth? £50, right? Its worth does not change.

In fact, even if it's so badly damaged it can't be used, the banks will exchange it for another — even destroyed it's worth £50.

Why do we assume that our worth declines with life's tough experiences? No matter what has happened or will happen, you are, and will remain, worthy; nothing changes that.

CHAPTER SUMMARY

- Worthiness is a solid state.
- It's something we talk ourselves out of feeling.
- Choose to place your crown of worthiness on your head.
- Even 'imperfect' people are worthy.
- Value and worth do not change based on your experience.

"I HAVE SO MUCH TO FEEL GRATEFUL FOR."

ESSENCE & ENERGY OF MONEY CARDS

31: ASK AND IT IS GIVEN

In this chapter, I cover how a verse from the Bible sums up manifesting money perfectly, and how to switch into the faith that it's true, so that you can bring what you want into your reality.

When I was about seven, I used to sing in the local church choir. Even at an early age I knew there had to be something more out there that we couldn't see, and I took myself along to the church and sang, and listened to the sermons. Although I never really connected with religion, it opened the door for me to explore that idea of 'something else'. I realised that religion is a form of spirituality and regardless of my thoughts and feelings about the Church or organised religion, I truly believe the stories, in their original form, which tell us how to use the Universal Laws. Of course, I focus on abundance, so the Law of Attraction is of particular interest to me. Religious texts from across the world have such striking similarities, all originating from a time when communication across the globe just wasn't possible.

Having gone to a church to find the 'something else', I heard stories of feeding the five thousand and turning water into wine, but the phrase that stuck in my head all these years was:

> *"Ask, and it shall be given you; seek, and ye shall find; knock, and it shall be opened unto you:"*

> *Matthew 7:7*

This is the ultimate description of the Law of Attraction and manifestation. It is the trust we need to create with money, the Universe and ourselves.

You might think 'I'm asking all the time', but are you asking with an open mind, heart and soul? With faith? Or are you asking only with your conscious mind and with doubt elsewhere.

What religion creates is faith. A deep-rooted belief that there is something more. When people feel into their religion, they are cultivating a relationship and learning to trust what can't be seen. Believing it's there even if sometimes it doesn't feel like it. It can take many years to feel the faith in a higher power.

My favourite thing about money alchemy is whilst you are building that faith in money, you are also creating that faith in yourself. Once you have that, (and it comes fast,) you become aware that not only can you ask for anything; but you can get it.

Money is very close to us, as you saw in chapter 26. It is everywhere. Money is always near us, because it's on this earth. Sometimes you'll ask, and it will be given so fast that you'll actually struggle to believe it. This happens a lot with my clients. The relationship with money can build quickly when you get your mind, body and soul in alignment. One way to do this is to ask the right questions, in the right way.

Have you ever seen something you want and thought 'It's too expensive' or 'I can't afford that?' Immediately, that shuts down any potential manifestation of the thing you want. As you'll remember from Chapter 28, it will likely also push it further away from you.

Instead try asking this question: What are the many ways I could manifest this? (then immediately surrendering it to money, The Universe, your higher self, God or whatever you believe in):

'Ask and it is given' is a true statement. You'll soon start to see all sorts of different ways you could bring what you desire towards you. You may even find it on your doorstep the very next day.

One of my clients told me about a coat which she fell in love with. She explained how beautiful it was, but that it was just so expensive and she had other priorities. She even told me she knew I was going to mention the language she used, but couldn't think of what to say instead. The fact that she couldn't afford it was true. How could she say anything else?

I shared with her the *Ask and It Is Given* verse, because that is also true, and she decided to ask 'How can I manifest this coat?' Immediately she noticed that she'd used the word 'how' and having worked with me for a while, said 'but you always tell me to get out of 'the how'. She's right! I explained that it's ok to ask for the how, you just need to get out of the way, once you have asked for it. We talked about some of the ways she could just let it go from her mind. She decided to release the how by writing it down and burning the paper it was written on.

The next day, my client voice messaged me squealing with delight. Her friend had seen the exact same coat in a charity shop, in great condition, and had bought it for her. She even dropped it off with my client, so it was delivered to her door the very next day. My client simply could not believe this had happened, and told me she could never, 'in a million years' have imagined it would come to her in that way.

Another client needed to manifest £2,000 immediately. We worked on releasing the need, asked in the form of writing a Magical Manifestation Cheque, and the money arrived in her account within a few hours. More joyful disbelief.

I'm a very slow, yet very steady manifester. I also very rarely have cash. Mark and I spent a weekend in Cornwall and I hadn't had any cash so for the whole time, I'd just used my cards. As we approached the Tamar bridge the signs said that the crossing was £2. It looked like they only took cash and Mark was a little panicked by this as he knew we didn't have any cash. I simply asked to locate £2 and sat for a moment as we approached the toll booth. I opened my purse and there was one £2 coin in it. I laughed out loud at this as it hadn't been there all weekend and yet there it was, ready for me to pass to Mark. Right when we needed it.

These may all seem like fairy stories, but they happen all the time when you ask the right questions and open up to faith in money. The so-called 'real world' can really block us though, and Mark is a great example of that. His mind went straight to the fact that it must have been there all the time. Maybe that's true, but I'd gone into my purse several times that weekend and didn't see any cash in there. Of course, Mark has the most logical explanation, but I choose to believe in magic. After all, that coat and that money which my clients manifested, weren't there all the time. Or were they?

Actually, I believe they were always there, just out of sight. You can manifest anything but your blocks, stories beliefs etc. can stop it, just as it gets to you. Focusing on needing to know the how rather than just asking how and letting it go, can mean you don't ever see it, even if it's right there in front of you.

Faith in money is knowing it's there for you, asking for it and then getting out of the way. There are only so many times something can be a coincidence. I now choose to see this as the magic of money alchemy.

CHAPTER SUMMARY

- You can manifest anything you ask for.
- Asking the right question can unblock your manifestations.
- The 'real world' can make you doubt your money magic.

"UNCOVERING YOUR MONEY STORY IS
THE KEY TO UNLOCKING ABUNDANCE."

32: YOUR MONEY STORY

In this chapter, I look at the origins of your money story and how it can trick you into believing you aren't worthy, or capable or deserving of more. Much of it is subconscious, some of it comes from past lives, but like any story you can rewrite it.

Your current money story is a combination of your lived experience, society's norms and beliefs that you have picked up along the way from parents, friends, teachers and other people.

Many of us have also brought parts of our money story from past lives, where we may have experienced similar patterns. In some cases, vows of poverty may even have been taken for a wide variety of reasons, but nearly always due to safety. These can also be brought into this lifetime.

Now, if these money stories have arisen through life or lives, what can you do about them? They seem very real, don't they? My own money story was based on many things, and I'm still unravelling where it all came from.

In past lives I have seen in the Akashic Records (a record of all thoughts and soul histories), I have had wealth, but was painfully lonely and sad. I've brought these feelings into this life for sure, and they have linked to a story of 'I can't be wealthy and happy'.

In this life, I was told, as many girls are, 'not to be too big for my boots' and 'you'll be brought down a peg or two'. I also learnt that I should not earn more than my parents. This was revealed when I was in my early twenties, and had got a new job. There was lots of interest until I was asked how much it paid. As soon as I said the number the topic changed and my work was never talked about again.

I didn't realise it at the time, but later it dawned on me that it was more than my parents earned. Maybe that was why the topic was changed? Maybe that was why I was never asked again?

I also had a real feeling of shame that evolved into a money block. For decades this shame would creep up on me. I could be driving around, thinking of nothing and suddenly I'd feel it, crawling up my body, painful and red. This shame was a lie that I told when I was five. I'd broken my dolls crib and blamed my friend. I'd seen this friend when we were in our thirties and I'd profusely apologised. She laughed because she didn't even remember the event. But still, the shame crept up on me at really random times.

In my early forties, I was so frustrated that even confessing and apologising hadn't helped that I went to a healer. I had Reiki to help release some of the shame and days later, as it continued to do its work, it hit me... "I'm not worthy". This was like a domino rally:

> **My "I'm not worthy list":**
> - "I'm not worthy because I told a lie when I was five."
> - "I'm not worthy because I grew up where I did."
> - "I'm not worthy because I have been divorced twice."
> - "I'm not worthy because I'm too tall or too short."
> - "I'm not worthy because I'm too much or not enough.
> - "I'm not worthy because I'm too shy or too bossy."
> - "I'm not worthy because if I was, life would be better for me."
> - "I'm not worthy because I didn't look after my pet rabbit as well as I could have."
> - "I'm not worthy because people don't help me even if I ask."

- "I'm not worthy because sometimes I think bad things."
- "I'm not worthy because I had a house repossessed."
- "I'm not worthy because I got into so much debt."
- "I'm not worthy because I could have prevented a lot of pain."

The list went on! And on! All starting with "I'm not worthy".

"I'm not worthy" often hides itself as other feelings and thoughts such as:
- "I can't be trusted."
- "I'm greedy."
- "I don't deserve."
- "I'm not good enough."
- "I'm not ready."
- "I'm not qualified enough."
- "I'm not unique enough."
- "I can't charge for my work."
- "I'm scared."
- ...and many, many others.

I was really surprised at how deep these all went, and just how much there was to heal. What's really interesting here, is that after some attempts to get involved in religion, I'd decided to follow my own path. Believing that everyone is worthy. That we simply need to rediscover that feeling and knowing. Yet, here I was, with a list, longer than my arm, of 'I'm not worthy' thoughts

I sat there, in floods of tears. Sadder than I'd ever been, mourning something I believed we all had, but a part of me just couldn't face or believe (and added 'I'm not worthy because I'm a hypocrite' to my long list). I saw myself as a little girl, alone with her teddy bear, in the dark, scared and afraid. In my mind I hugged that little girl, I spoke kindly to her and cried with her.

Now, many of my 'I'm not worthy' thoughts don't even seem to link to money, but the core belief behind it is; you've guessed it; I'm not worthy. This is my money story, and there are lots of events and experiences that created it within me. Even though I know my worthiness does not change, my money story tricked me into believing it did. You see, the work with money alchemy is so much more than just being about money. As I've mentioned before, it's about your relationship with yourself and being able to trust yourself.

Should we associate self-worth with money? Of course not. Do we? Hell yes! So, let's work with it rather than against it. Money is the route back to belief in our worth; not because money makes us worthy or proves our worth, but because, money as a feminine being, teaches us to be kind to ourselves. She teaches us to like ourselves, and then to love ourselves. And as a result of that, the feeling of worth is remembered and reignited, and abundance flows.

'Remember' is the word here. I believe that this work is a reminder for our souls. It's not new knowledge. It's something we've forgotten. It's something we've shut off in ourselves and instead we walk in circles and cycles of struggle and stress. Partly because it wasn't safe at times in our past/pasts, and partly because that's how we roll in today's society. The media feeds us doom and gloom, our friends and family feed us doom and gloom, and as a result we feel that doom and gloom too.

When you feel something you are powerfully creating it. Therefore, more doom and gloom gets created, and we see that as proof that it is the only reality. But when you remember there's a different way of being, you create that too.

Now, I'm not saying that my way is all roses and butterflies. The truth is, sometimes life is hard. It throws us curve balls and it hurts. Life isn't about getting through it untouched. But that does not impact our worthiness in any way.

Money stories are a huge topic. It can take a long time to uncover all of the pieces of yours. Mine are still revealing themselves to me. I've learned to be inquisitive and come at them with a sense of humour.

162

Sometimes that is extra challenging, and the sadness that I've carried this stuff with me can be really heavy.

Opening up to having more money and abundance in your life, is a journey of shifting your perceptions from scarcity to expansiveness. However, that doesn't mean you shouldn't feel other feelings. Ideally, you want to feel high vibration feelings. But, to get to that point, and in order to genuinely feel those, you do first need to go through some hard and heavy feelings. Then, you can heal and return to those high vibe feelings.

As part of my process, I hold pity parties for myself. I'll run a bath and I'll sit and cry or feel the junky heavy stuff. I'll mourn what could have been if only I hadn't had that story or belief, or had broken the pattern sooner. I sometimes feel cross at myself for not seeing it earlier, or for even allowing that belief to seem real. But when I pull the plug, I visualise all that negativity and heaviness flowing out of the bath with the water. At that point, the pity party is over. I'll take as long as I need, but have an end time in mind — sometimes it's half an hour, other times it's two hours. During this time, I feel my feelings in all their misery. But when the time I've set is over, it's time to start moving forward.

Think of your money story as an operating system, such as you would find on your phone or computer. It's a bunch of coding that has worked well for a long time. But things move on and upgrades are needed. After a while, if you don't upgrade the system, things start to break and glitch. You know it should work, but for some reason you just can't get it to.

When it comes to money, you'll find that you get to the point, where you know money can and will be easy for you. You understand that building a relationship with money is the key, and you try to get things moving. But you hit huge resistance and find you get tripped up. This is a sign your money programming needs an upgrade. Upgrades are needed fairly regularly, as you add more and more knowledge and learning to it. Sometimes upgrades can cause glitches whilst they settle. We've all experienced this with our phones, I'm sure. It can be a little odd while you get used to the new way of working, but eventually it becomes normal. It's time to upgrade the programming, and change the story that's in your head, heart and soul.

It's often easy to change the story in your head. You see something different that works and you can get on board with that. In your head you know what you want to change i.e., to have more money without the struggle. Unless you have your heart and soul aligned with your head though, your old programming and story will creep back in through negative self-talk, doubt and self-sabotage.

CHAPTER SUMMARY

- You won't know what your money story is, until you look for it.
- It's coloured your feelings of worth, value and deserving.
- You can upgrade or change your money story, and open up to creating a new one.

"I KNOW MY VALUE AND AM COMFORTABLE
GETTING PAID FOR IT."

ESSENCE & ENERGY OF MONEY CARDS

33: CHARGING FOR YOUR SPIRITUAL GIFTS

In this chapter, I explore why charging is an important part of your work if you have a spiritual business. The same principles apply across all businesses and employment. You should charge for your skills, talents, knowledge and impact.

'You shouldn't charge for your gifts. They must be shared with the world for free!' This is such a common phrase in the spiritual community and it is often stated by people who don't charge for their gifts. They believe that no one should charge for their gifts (or only get paid travelling expenses). To that I say 'I'm sorry, what?'

In no other industry, are decades of learning and development so underrated, yet expected. I fail to see the difference between your spiritual gift development and going to university to become a marketer, lawyer, teacher, whatever.

The fact is that very few of us are naturals at mediumship, healing and other spiritual gifts. Yes, we may have a more natural tendency (otherwise seen by society as talent, such as with gifted football players, and leaders) but even if that so-called talent is present, it still has to be developed. This development often takes much longer than it takes to get a degree or many other qualifications.

I got my first inkling that I had 'something' when I was five. I knew I could fly! I also knew it wasn't actually flying. It was an ability to see things as if I was flying up above them. I didn't know what it meant, and I thought everyone had this ability. Later in my teens, I came across the first ever witch that I consciously recognised as such (although I realise now that there were many before her). She was my foster mother and when I got in from school, she'd sit me in the lounge with the Tarot cards and make me draw meaning from them. No guide book, no explanation. It was hard, and I hated it at first. She was teaching me to reconnect with my intuition. Very soon I was an exceptional reader. A few years later, I gave a reading to someone who was a sceptic and wanted to test me. I found myself flying above his life. I saw his mother and him. I saw things he'd never told anyone in his life. What felt like a few seconds later, I came back to Earth, and saw him with his mouth wide open and tears in his eyes.

I'd been reading for more than 40 minutes and had relayed clear proof from his past (not something I'd ever been taught to do) and made predictions that made absolute sense to him regarding the present and future. Despite this being a huge success, I was terrified. I'd lost all connection to time and reality during that reading. I didn't understand it. I wasn't just reading the cards; I was acting as a medium. That day, I packed away my cards and didn't touch them again for over 20 years.

For this reason, I don't believe any spiritual gift is easy to develop. No spiritual gift should be undervalued. It takes tenacity, repetition, time, courage and a lot of overcoming of fear and doubt. People who say you should give your gifts for free are, quite frankly, wrong and don't value what you bring.

Many people have gifts or talents, and they still need to develop them. You wouldn't expect a marketing expert to work for free, or a lawyer. They worked hard to develop their skills, right? Well, so did you! Why should you be expected to work for free? Now, maybe you feel like you can charge for your gifts, but how much?

Many of my clients have what I call 'going-rate-itis' when they come to me. They look around at other people offering the same service in the area, and see that as the ceiling to what they can charge; the going rate. Then they start comparing themselves to others, how long they've been doing what they do, how many courses they've done and who they've trained with, then add that junk into the pricing. They can't move on from that, and because everyone is looking at everyone else before they know it, ten years have passed and they're still charging the same amount. Even though the value of money has gone down.

What's worse is that they don't feel particularly valued by some of their clients. This starts to eat away at the joy of their work, and can even lead to them stopping altogether. People *need* your work!

Your prices often reflect two things:

- your money story
- the story you tell yourself about what your clients can afford

---

If you wouldn't pay more than £60 for, let's say, a card reading, you aren't going to be able to charge more for your own card reading service. There are many potential clients out there who would actually look at £60 for a card reading and think 'Ooo, that's a bit steep' or 'That's a good price' or 'Oh no, that's way too cheap — I bet they aren't that good'. The thing is, everyone is right, based on their beliefs and views.

I remember when I was selling flamingo and unicorn gifts as one of my first businesses. I was at an artisan market and I had, among other things, flamingo watering cans. They were priced at £18. A woman walked past, picked it up and told me that it was 'way too expensive and you probably should lower your prices if you want to sell anything'. It knocked me. I wobbled after she'd left. Not more than six minutes later (although it felt like a lifetime as I stood there doubting myself), another woman came along and exclaimed 'Oh my god! These are a bargain, I'll take three'.

This was a huge learning point for me. Your price is your price. Some people will think you are expensive, but what they're actually saying is that they don't value what you are offering. This may be because you haven't demonstrated your product or skill well enough or perhaps just because that's what they believe. Others will take three at the same price that was too expensive for some. They see your value.

Now, which of these two types of clients would you prefer to work with?

I'm going to take the ones who see my value, and don't even think to question my prices.

When I first started out, I really did struggle over what I should charge. But if I'm honest, I put a huge amount of energy into what I thought my clients could and couldn't afford. Kendall Summerhawk, one of my early coaches would often say 'Get out of your client's wallet'. It took me sometime to realise what she meant by this, but here's what I saw: frequently, the people who said yes to my offer were those that I thought wouldn't be able to afford it. I realised I had no idea what their finances were like and I'd made some pretty big assumptions, which were actually very misaligned and misinformed.

I also saw people who would tell me they desperately needed to work with me but couldn't afford me, then go on to buy things like game consoles for their kids, 5-star holidays and new cars. I found this quite confusing at first, but I soon realised that this was about priorities. We can often find money for things that are super important to us, even in a pinch. But things that aren't so important, we struggle to find money for. Money really is magical. These potential clients were not lying. They didn't have the money to work with me, because it simply wasn't a priority for them, even though they thought it was. And that is totally ok.

For every person who thinks your prices are high, there'll be others who think your prices are too low. Having lower prices often turns people off, more so even than having higher prices. There is a whole range of clients out there who are happy to pay more for what you offer. You may have seen people in your field charging hundreds or even thousands more than you do. Does it trigger you? It used to trigger me.

I've done some work with a holistic coach who used to charge £35 per session, yet despite this low price she struggled to find clients. She increased her prices and now charges £170 per session. As soon as she did this, she had more clients booked in within two days than she had seen in the last two months. On top of that, her clients show up open and ready to work and they give raving reviews.

Yes, some people think she is outrageously priced while others can't afford her. Many of her clients save and save to work with her. People who pay are more attentive and are much more open. I've found that people who don't pay, or just pay lower prices, are the biggest sceptics. They don't expect things to work for them and as there's very little commitment on their part, they don't.

Money creates a flow of energy and the more energy that flows, the more committed people are to maintaining that flow and benefiting from it. People who pay are way more open to results.

Now, I'm not telling you to put up your prices, I'm asking you to think about what you charge. Are you being caught up in the narrative that you shouldn't charge, or charge well, for your gifts? Are you suffering from going-rate-itis? Are you getting in your clients' wallets and assuming you know what their priorities are? Are your clients connected and committed to the energy flow when they show up?

CHAPTER SUMMARY

- Charging for your gifts, skills and knowledge can feel icky.
- Not charging, damages the impact of your work.
- You are worthy of being paid well for your work.
- Going-rate-itis places an illusory ceiling on your pricing.
- The right people will be happy to pay you, and to pay you well.

"I FORGIVE MY MONEY PAST."

ESSENCE & ENERGY OF MONEY CARDS

34: HEALING YOUR MONEY PAST

In this chapter, I share some really powerful ways to heal your past when it comes to money. Using a combination of them all will help release deep blocks and even money wounds, and this will open up the flow of abundance and money toward you.

The first thing to remember when it comes to healing your money blocks, is that you don't need fixing. Think of a time when you almost lost your balance. Your mind and body reacted together. You likely felt a feeling in your tummy or solar plexus. You regained your balance and carried on.

With a money block, your mind simply doesn't allow you to carry on down that path. It is much too scary. Now, with your new understanding of money, you've regained that balance and can move forward.

These methods of healing are ways of getting that balance or perspective back. First, you'll need to release that feeling of unbalance. That will come in the form of energetic releases. These are powerful, physical releases.

If you were to ever see one of my live group coaching sessions, you'd see my wonderful clients yawning their heads off. It's not because they're bored or tired. It's because they are regaining balance and releasing the energy that has held them back. Sometimes, when I'm doing healing with them one to one, there are coughs, throat tickles, burps, tears, sobs and even swearing. All of these physical releases are evidence of energy shifting. Don't hold it in, just allow it to release. You will feel lighter when you do.

The very first, and I think, most powerful healing technique when it comes to money is awareness. This is so underrated, but as I've mentioned before, by simply becoming aware that you have a block can be 80% of the work. As you've been reading this book you've probably had many moments of awareness, so you are already on your way to healing these.

Sometimes, I felt cross with myself for letting these things happen. and for not seeing them sooner. If you feel like this, remember that you didn't know what you didn't know. Now you do, you can change it.

When I feel I'm being harsh with myself I turn to self-forgiveness. It isn't always easy but the method I use really helps. When I was trained as a belief clearing practitioner, this method was covered only briefly, but it is a gentle and powerful approach.

Ho'oponopono is a beautiful Hawaiian practice and prayer for forgiveness. There is a lot that we don't know about it, and I'm certainly no expert, but it helps you to let go of the things you would benefit from letting go of.

The part of the process I use is the four-line prayer:

> *I'm sorry*
> *Please forgive me*
> *Thank you*
> *I love you*

I say this to myself, in my head whilst I'm feeling resistance to letting my blocks go, and being hard on myself. I'm always so surprised at how different I feel after just a few rounds of it.

Try it. And if you love it, I highly recommend diving deeper into the beautiful practice. There are loads of books and videos on it.

Journaling is also a very powerful money block clearing tool. I have a really on/off relationship with journaling myself, but I am a huge advocate of it because, quite simply, it works.

So how do you journal when it comes to money? I write down the block I want to work through at the top of my page and sit with it for a minute, and then I write. I normally cry as I write, or get angry, but by the time I've finished, that's all gone, and I feel renewed.

Now, journaling can be a sticking point for some, so here's some tips to get it flowing.

How to get in the journaling flow

- Decide what you are going to do with it before you start. I like to burn my pages as a further release (make sure you do this safely). You might want to shred it, or bury it. I don't recommend keeping your journal pages because you want to let it all go. This type of journaling is for healing rather than looking back at your life over time. Getting rid of it also means you never have to worry about someone else reading it. It's just for you.

- If you can't think of something to write, write anything. My client, Sharon, told me she writes the word 'rhubarb' over and over until words start to flow. When your writing is blocked, the healing can't happen; so, this excellent tip gets you writing. It also makes you laugh when you're writing it, and that's healing in itself. You will find your feelings and writing will start to flow if you put pen to paper and go through the motions.

- Don't judge yourself as you write. Just allow it to come out. I've written some really harsh things and I've come to realise this is my wound speaking, not me. I don't even read mine back now. For me, the magic is in the doing. It doesn't matter if your writing doesn't make sense, or has spelling mistakes, or is unintelligible in places. It was never about writing well; it was about healing well.

With my clients, I also use two other healing modalities: Emotional Freedom Technique, also known as tapping and a form of Rapid Energy Release treatment called Silent Counselling. Both of these involve tapping or touching specific points on the body to release trapped energy and realign it in a positive way. They both work wonderfully, and frankly the results are just magical.

These are just some of the ways you can heal your money stories and blocks and change your beliefs. There are many more too. I've found this combination to be the most effective, both for my own healing and that of my clients.

Healing is an ongoing thing, because beliefs and wounds are often multi-layered. Sometimes you'll notice a familiar block and it's easy to feel like the work you have done hasn't had an impact, but it has. Think of this work as a never ending upward spiral. You may find yourself looking at the same thing, but you are on the next level this time.

Healing takes work, effort and energy but as with all things money, it's always worth it. Make sure you rest and are kind to yourself when you do your healing work. Pick a time of day that is just for you. You may feel a little tired, so nap when you can.

CHAPTER SUMMARY

- Healing your money story can be done in many ways.
- Awareness is the bulk of the work.
- You will likely experience physical releases, as you do this work.
- Journaling and self-forgiveness help to release emotions that are stuck.
- There are other forms of energy release that go even deeper and work faster.

"MONEY SUPPORTS ME."

ESSENCE & ENERGY OF MONEY CARDS

35: HAVING A HEALTHY RELATIONSHIP WITH MONEY

In this chapter, I revisit some of the principles that warrant repeating, so that you can create something beautiful and healthy in your relationship with money. It is a relationship, and that means it needs a bit of work every now and then. Even the easiest of relationships need this.

Think of your connection with money as a relationship. Just like all relationships, there's that wonderful phase when you've just met. You're so energised by each other and see only the most amazing things together. Over time this fades, and whether you want to or not, you will start taking your partner for granted. It happens with money too.

You'll be in the throes of loving money and having her in your life, but over time you'll stop putting as much work in. Your money magic foundations will get forgotten, and your relationship will start to feel strained.

You'll notice this, and commit to putting in more effort to go back to seeing, paying attention, making space, speaking kindly of and appreciating money, and your relationship will improve. This will repeat, and this is why 'getting back on the bus' is a chapter in this book.

Money won't hold it against you, ever. She's there with open arms, just waiting to reconnect with you. The foundations will help you do this and they will also reconnect you to your relationship with yourself.

This is all normal and I wanted to write this short chapter as a reminder of that. This is such an important relationship to build and nurture in your lifetime, but there will be times when you don't. The important thing is that you recognise it.

A healthy relationship isn't a perfect one. It's one with acceptance, love and support. It's knowing that you aren't perfect and don't need to be. You just need to keep going. In a healthy relationship there's no blame or shame. There's just no need for those.

You will see clear parallels in your own relationships too, not just with money or yourself. I remember thinking this was a weird thing to say when I first heard it:

"The way you do money is the way you do everything."

Kendall Summerhawk

The more you look, the more you'll realise this is true. Your diet, your family, your friends, your work, all reflect the way you do money. You may even have noticed that the money magic foundations are not just powerful money habits, they are habits for life.

Remember that the more you put into your relationship with money, the more you'll get out. Not just more money, but more everything. You'll feel more confident and be so much kinder to yourself. You'll see abundance of all sorts everywhere. You'll be able to manifest on demand and with ease. Is that worth a bit of effort? I truly believe it is.

I'm still on this journey. It's a practice, a deliberate focus on something better, something more than you've been taught you can have. It's exciting and yet you'll still forget it sometimes. That's ok. Just get started again, hop back on the bus and travel with money, rather than without her.

CHAPTER SUMMARY

- Creating a healthy relationship with money does need a little work, just like any healthy relationship does.
- The money magic foundations give you core things to focus on.
- The way you are in your relationship with money shows up in all aspects of your life.
- You aren't perfect and that's ok, as money doesn't expect you to be.

"I ADD VALUE EVERYDAY WITH MY SKILLS, ABILITIES AND UNIQUENESS."

ESSENCE & ENERGY OF MONEY CARDS

36: TOOLS FOR MANIFESTING MORE MONEY

In this chapter, I explain just some of the tools you can use to help supercharge your money work and manifestations. I am a little obsessed with all of these, but I find they help me to be clear on my intentions and let go of the how. Feel free to add in your own.

I was taught to use tools for magic and manifestations very early on in my spiritual education. After shutting it all down for decades, to fit in, it was crystals, oils and cards that got me opening up again. They are tools for strengthening your focus, your intention and your connection. I believe you don't actually need any of these tools, but I know how much joy they bring to me when I use them, and that joyfulness adds extra magic into the mix.

Although these tools have given meanings, it's really important to draw your own meaning from them too. Just because I work with these in this way, doesn't mean you can't use different tools or apply completely different ways, as you want to, that's fine too.

In the next few pages, we'll go on a very short whistle-stop tour. If you'd like to find out more about any of these tools, check out the book resources, near the end of this book for a list of helpful information:

1. CRYSTALS

Crystals are amazing tools for working with money. On a magical level they each have different frequencies, hence the different colours, structure and feel. They are programmable based on your desires.

On a more practical level they are great for anchoring in things you want to feel and achieve. They serve as amazing reminders each day to connect with yourself and money. Plus, as an added bonus, they look amazing. I have to admit to having a small (ok, maybe not so small) addiction to buying crystals. I feel like they call me and I work with different crystals throughout the year, for different things.

When it comes to money, as a topic, there are crystals that I recommend to get you started. As you progress and start to feel the healing happening, you'll be drawn to others for different reasons.

If you are just starting out with crystals, don't feel overwhelmed or confused. There are loads of amazing resources and people who can help, and as with most of this work, go with what you feel. Your intuition will guide you, even if you don't understand it at the time. Know that crystals want to work with you, and even if you just think they are pretty and don't yet feel their magic, they will be there for you.

Key crystals for manifesting money	
Citrine	A yellow (sometimes slightly greenish) clear crystal. This crystal is known to support the drawing of prosperity and wealth towards you. Simple and powerful, I have these all around my house and in coat pockets to serve as reminders of what I am manifesting.
Iron pyrite	Also known as Fool's Gold. This bright and shiny crystal is fascinating to look at. Its structure is of tiny (although sometimes larger) cubes and it is the colour of gold. It's like a ray of sunshine and of all of the crystals, I find this one extremely energetic! It

	'tingles' when I hold it! It's so opulent looking, and you simply can't help but be reminded of the wonder of money, when using it.
Green aventurine	A gorgeous green, one of the colours of money. It is gentle and cleansing. A crystal that's great for supporting you as you open your heart to money as a feminine being. It's all well and good being able to manifest with the other stones, but if you aren't feeling that connection to money, you may find it hard to see or hold onto. Green aventurine will help you.

Here's some advice on how to use your crystals. Crystals absorb energy from their surroundings so it's a good idea to cleanse and charge them. Don't worry, it doesn't take long and I think you'll love the process. Again, there are many amazing resources and people out there who can help you take this further. I'm sharing my practice here so you can get started straight away.

Cleansing and charging can be done with any of the four alchemical elements Fire (we use smoke), Earth, Water and Air. It can also be done with the moon, other crystals and salt. Pick the one that feels right for you. I choose the fast ones because I'm impatient.

Fire	Burn some incense and pass the crystal through the smoke for several minutes.
Earth	Wrap the crystals in a tea towel and bury in the ground for a week or longer (you might want to do this on a specific moon phase if you feel drawn to it). Top Tip — place a marker above ground so you don't lose your crystals.
Water	This should only be used for certain crystals; the ones listed above are fine to cleanse with water. Other crystals may disintegrate in water. Pour water,

	preferably spring water or river water, over your crystals. Let sit for a few minutes then air dry.
Air	My favourite. I have a gorgeous shamanic feather fan which I use to waft air over my crystals to cleanse them. You can use your hands to do this or even the wind.
Full moon	I lay all of my crystals out on the lawn on the night of a full moon and leave them overnight. Only do this with crystals that won't be damaged by water, in case it rains or there is a dew.
Selenite	This crystal looks like pure moonlight; you can charge your crystals by laying them on Selenite.
Salt	Bury your crystal in a pot of salt; use natural rock or sea salt. Leave buried for a few hours.

Now your crystals are ready:

- Hold each one in your hand and notice it, really notice it.
- As you hold it, think of what you'd like it to represent and help to bring toward you. Hold that thought, and imagine the thought going into the crystal. After a few moments, you can let go and do the same with the others.

Here's what I think of and programme my crystals with:

My citrine	*"Remind me that money is all around me, that I am manifesting all the time and that I am abundant."*
My pyrite	*"Being abundant is a wonderful feeling. I am uplifted and reminded of the beauty and energy that money and abundance brings to me."*

My green aventurine	*"My heart is open to receive the abundance I draw towards me. Money and abundance is joy and love."*

What I love the most about my crystals, is that they are always around me. I often notice them more when my relationship with money is getting a little shaky. They serve as a wonderful reminder to reconnect with myself and the magic of money. They work in the background whilst you are going about your day, and pop up right when you need them. I can't explain it any better than that. They just are wonderful to have around.

As mentioned earlier, science has been aware of their power in many ways, for a long time. They have been used throughout history to convey messages and meaning and to serve as protection. Often crystals are a first step into the magical world, just outside our logical and very structured reality. They can open the door to another way of being.

2. OILS.

I use essential oils as they capture the essence and energy of the plant they have been extracted from; but I always dilute them with a high-quality carrier oil such as jojoba (which is a gorgeous golden colour).

Essential oils are powerful in many ways, and this makes them perfect for money alchemy work.

My favourite oil for money work is wild orange. This gorgeous citrus oil is extracted from the skin of the orange and has a really grounding yet ethereal feel. To me this is how I know my Money Goddess is near. I'm grounded but I'm also connected to the Universe. It also triggers a wonderful memory of driving in Portugal, seeing the orange trees heaving under the abundance of big, ripe oranges as the sun set. There were orange trees as far as the eye could see. Total abundance. My clients love it too and it's part of the preparation for money alchemy work.

I tend to use a cold-water diffuser to fill the air with an amazing scent, and prepare myself to do some amazing transformations with money.

Over time, and as I've come to know myself much more, I've been drawn to many other oils. Spikenard, myrtle and violet have helped me significantly on my journey with money, but for very different reasons. Spikenard showed me how powerful and strong my manifestations can be. Myrtle helped me overcome fears around visibility and violet helped me process grief that was holding me back.

The wild orange oil seems to be loved by everyone for money work, so if you were looking for an oil, I'd recommend starting there. The others will be down to your preference and your connection to them will develop over time. Choose oils that you 'feel'. That invoke something inside of you.

Before I use an oil for the first time, I connect with it by holding the bottle in my hand and just see if I can sense something from it. Sometimes I can, other times I can't, but this moment is a great way to respectfully ask the oil to work with you. Be careful with the oils, whichever you use. Some oils can really irritate the skin, so always follow the instructions on the bottle.

3. TAROT AND ORACLE CARDS

When I was in my teens, my foster mother taught me how to read tarot cards. Now these aren't for everyone, for many reasons, but there are many amazing alternatives now, which if you are concerned about Tarot, offer a really powerful option. My favourites are oracle cards and affirmation cards. Oracle cards are great for longer messages and guidance, and are often beautifully illustrated. They come with a guide book so you can find out what each card means, without being a card reader as such. Affirmation cards are simple cards, with statements on them to challenge and inspire you.

When I realised that there isn't a huge range of money based cards out there, I was drawn to create my own deck: *The Essence & Energy Of Money Cards.* (I've shared details of these in the resources page near the back of this book if you'd like to know more about them.)

I'm not going to go into how to use these for readings (as that's a whole other book), just how to use them for money manifesting. It's really simple.

Choose your deck, shuffle and whilst you do so, ask a question. It can be any question, but preferably not one with a Yes/No response. I often just ask 'What do I need to know today?' Keep shuffling until a card falls out. And it will! Sometimes several will fall out, and this is the cards giving you even more guidance.

Review the image, and words and sit with the guidance for a moment. See if anything comes up. If it does, act on it. If not, be open to the message becoming clearer as the day passes.

I then display my card on a mini easel so that I'm reminded of it throughout the day. I also place one on my money altar when working on something big.

4. MAGICAL MANIFESTATION CHEQUES

I first came across writing cheques from the Universe in Rhonda Byrne's book, *The Magic*. I immediately loved the concept of them but struggled to make them work for me. I'm a slow and steady manifester and I love consistency, so manifesting chunks of money sounded wonderful to me, but I didn't have faith in my abilities to do it. Of course, now I know different, but back then I didn't. I decided to tailor the approach for my own style of manifesting, and started writing cheques monthly.

These are blank cheques that you write to yourself, from the Universe. They are a great way of setting money goals and intentions. My goodness they work well. Even when they don't pay they give you something. This is my favourite way to manifest money, and my clients love it too.

The cheques are the most valuable pieces of paper you will ever hold in your hands. Because they are literally blank cheques that can create your desires with you.

At first, I really struggled with this tool. My first cheque was for £3,000. It didn't get paid. I wrote another the following month, for the same amount, and it didn't get paid either. The third month, it got paid, I made £3,000 in my business for the very first time. What was fascinating though, was when I looked back at the first two cheques that didn't get paid, I'd actually made more money than I ever had in my business before. Just not the £3,000. In other words, the cheques that didn't get paid, got me closer and closer.

After that first cheque got paid, I wrote two more for the same amount, and they got paid too. I started to feel a bit confident so I doubled the number and crashed and burned.

What happened? I got confident consciously, but subconsciously I was freaking out. I ended up in the how and stressed myself out so much I almost quit my business and applied for a job. Money block alert! It was the worst month I'd ever experienced in terms of income. This was such a gift though. I realised that I had sensed something when I wrote it, but ignored it.

This was when I truly discovered the sweet spot for manifesting money. I call it the *money tension*.

Before I explain this, I want to make it clear that you are capable of manifesting whatever amount of money you desire. I was more than capable of manifesting the double amount I wrote on that cheque, but here's the thing...

When you have money blocks, beliefs and patterns that hold you back, your subconscious feels unsafe manifesting that amount, and will create events and situations that stop it coming to you; or pushes it straight away from you. When you overwhelm your subconscious, you're back at the base of the mountain looking up, wanting to do it but freaking out about it. You must have a tiny glimmer of belief.

Can you write cheques for £1billion? Of course you can!

Will you connect with it enough to make it an intention? Probably not. That's where it falls down.

Money tension is the feeling of your intention or money goal being just in the realm of possibility, right now for you. It takes practice to feel it, just as the cheques take practice. It's all a practice that needs to be repeated and refined, so don't feel put off if it takes some time to figure it out. You will.

If you write down a number and your mind instantly says, 'Ha ha, like that's ever going to happen', you don't have money tension. If you write down a number and your mind says 'Easy, we've done it before', again, you don't have money tension. The sweet spot is when you write a number and your mind says 'Interesting! I'm not sure how, but I guess it might be possible'.

Over the years, I've written many Magical Manifestation Cheques. Now about 80% to 90% get paid. I'm writing cheques for amounts I couldn't even say without laughing out loud just a few years ago, and I'm writing them every month.

This is not a linear process; my cheques don't just go up each month. I feel into the money tension, and sometimes I feel the need to write a slightly lower cheque amount, other times I stay at the same amount for a while. I like consistency to prove things are real. I feel the money tension and go with what that tells me.

As I mentioned, it takes practice to feel the tension, so if you can't yet feel it, just add up your existing income and add 10%. Notice what thoughts and feelings that figure creates and use this as your starting point.

The key is to not focus on the cheque throughout the month. Look at it often, but don't focus on it. When you focus on it, the how starts to creep back in. Let it *cook* away in the background, where you can see it, and *allow* it to work rather than trying to *make* it work.

At the end of the month, look everywhere and add up the income. Work out if it has been paid. If it has, congratulations! Do a crazy happy dance and send gratitude to money.

If it hasn't? Congratulations too! Money has something to show you.

What money is showing you:

- The number didn't have the right money tension. It was too big or too small, but either way, you were disconnected from it.
- Your income may be increasing, even if the whole number didn't get paid, this means it's on its way. The how is likely to have got in the way a bit.
- You have a block somewhere that needs a little bit of work.

So, what do you do when this happens? As with the paid cheque, you send gratitude to money for showing you something. Most importantly, you write a new cheque. Do this every month. Keep going. It is a practice that takes fine tuning over time. You will see results if you take action and write the cheques.

There is a really powerful way to remove limits on your manifestations with these amazing cheques. The Universe may have even more to send to you, than what you asked for. So, when you set your number, simply add 'or more' after it. I completely forgot about this magic tip when I started, and when my cheques paid out, the amount was really close to the amount I'd asked for. The first time I added 'or more' to my intention on my cheque, it paid out *plus* an extra 50%.

Now, cheques are a big topic so in the resources page, near the back of this book, you'll find my training on how to write these and get them working for you.

CHAPTER SUMMARY

- Crystals, oils and cards are great tools to add to your money alchemy work.
- Allow them to mean what they mean to you.
- Take time to connect with your tools.
- Remember to check out the resources page near the end of the book to get started with Magical Manifestation Cheques.

"HEALING CAN BE PAINFUL AND BUMPY,
BUT IT'S ALWAYS WORTH IT."

37: WHAT DO SPOTS AND MONEY HAVE IN COMMON?

In this chapter, I will explain what can happen when you start working on your relationship with money. Most of the side effects of money alchemy are amazing, so this one may be a little bit of a shock. Don't worry though, it's an important part of the clearing process and it passes fast.

I'm going to go a little off topic for a bit here, but bear with me, there is a point, I promise.

Have you ever changed your skincare routine? Maybe you decided to look after your skin more, and added in some products, or maybe you changed an already decent routine to make it even better.

You diligently carry out your routine, day and night, with your new products and your skin feels amazing. Until, a week or so later you think you can see a spot, or a blemish. Then another one appears... what's going on?

Your skin is often adjusting to your new routine and having a breakout. The spots and blemishes will pass as your skin settles into this new approach. It sucks, but it happens and it passes.

This can happen with money too. You start doing all the right things, you're doing the money magic foundations, you're working on your relationship with money, you're feeling good and then a big bill lands on the door mat. It sucks. You may even feel like yelling 'What's the point?' You've made the changes, you've got a new money routine and then that bill lands. That bill is your spot. You may have a few of these spots appear shortly after you make the changes but it's so important to see them for what they are. This is money's way of clearing out the gunk that's underneath the surface. This is what has been hiding, or more likely what you've been avoiding, and once you have seen them and dealt with them, this breakout will clear.

It can feel really sucky, but this is evidence that the money alchemy is starting to work. Part of the alchemy process is the coming apart of the old ways and the coming together of the new way of being. It can be a bit painful and a bit bumpy, but when it does come back together fully, it's different. Just like your relationship with money will be.

So rather than seeing these breakouts as a sign to stop doing the work, see them as proof it's working. Even if it is sucky, it'll be worth it.

CHAPTER SUMMARY

- Money breakouts can happen when you start doing the work.
- Think of this as your spots after changing your skincare routine.
- It can suck!
- It's proof that the work you are doing is working.

"YOU CANNOT SERVE FROM AN EMPTY VESSEL."

ELEANOR BROWN

38: GIVE ONLY FROM YOUR SAUCER

In this chapter, I look at why trying to 'give from an empty cup', or even a full cup, is not helping you or others, and what to do instead. This applies to money, but also to every aspect of your life as abundance can be time, energy and health too.

You've probably heard the phrase 'you can't give from an empty cup' and know that it means you shouldn't give your time, energy, attention and help, when you don't have any for yourself. As women, we are often guilty of doing this. There are so many people relying on you and if you don't do it then who will? This leads to feeling guilty for taking a nap and feeling like going to the toilet, without a kid or cat in tow, is somehow a treat.

With money, this approach can find you lending or giving money away, when you really don't have enough yourself. In business it looks like being an over-giver when it comes to your time, and not putting yourself first.

The thing is, if you give from an empty cup, you aren't giving the person receiving the very best of you. Often this leads to resentment of the other person or yourself for not being recognised for the amount of effort it took for you to give what you gave.

Even if you give from a full cup, you are depleting yourself and taking away from what you have; although it feels a little easier and better than giving when you are empty, it still creates a problem for you. You need to find a way to refill it.

I recommend to all my clients that they only give from their saucer, their overflow and their abundance. That way your cup never needs refilling. You have everything you need and can give from a totally full and abundant place whether you are giving money, time, energy or anything else. When you give from your saucer, you'll find you feel much less taken for granted, and you'll never feel depleted.

This can be really hard when you first start doing it, and you may feel a little selfish. But, remember that when you give from abundance, or your saucer, you show up for people, not just with what you have left, but with more, so much more.

If you keep giving from your cup, you can't give or help as much, or as well as you want to. Plus, if your cup breaks you suffer and so does everyone else you help and support. The overflow means the cup is always more than full, and you therefore have even more to give, if you want to.

So, the next time someone asks for something from you, whether it's money, time, energy or something else, check in with yourself. Ask yourself this question:

'Do I have an overflow in my saucer to give from?'

If yes, go for it if you want to.

If no, ask yourself 'Am I willing and able to refill what this will take away from me'.

This question may seem harsh, but when you don't have an overflow in your saucer there is going to be an impact, and it is important to know if that impact is something you want to deal with.

If you say yes to this question, that's fine, you've thought it through. Most of the time we just give and give and never consider the consequences. This is why you should always ask yourself this question.

If you say no, then the answer is either 'No.' (which, by the way, is a complete sentence and something I often need reminding of) or 'I can't right now but ask me again in a month' or similar.

Not giving your time, money and energy can often be as wonderful a feeling as giving. This is part of your new relationship with yourself.

CHAPTER SUMMARY

- Giving from an empty cup puts a lot of things at risk.
- Even giving from a full cup has consequences for you.
- Aim to only give from your saucer, the overflow.
- Become aware of where you are giving from.

"I DESERVE ABUNDANCE, HAPPINESS AND WEALTH."

ESSENCE & ENERGY OF MONEY CARDS

39: TRANSFORMING INTO WEALTH

In this chapter, I explain what transforming into wealth is, the importance of doing this and why you might not be as far away from it as you think you are.

Transforming into wealth is something you have already started doing, just by picking up this book. Each chapter you read gives you a new way of thinking about money, and shows you where you might have blocks that are holding you back. This transformation will continue if you continue to do the money alchemy work.

Sometimes the transformations are subtle. You might find yourself comfortable and happy to pay £100 for something which you would never have considered before. You may find that your values around money have changed, and that it's important rather than just plain necessary. You will probably find yourself worrying less about money. That's part of the transformation into wealth.

I used to think that wealth was a number, but it's actually a freedom; a freedom, for example, from the stress and sleepless nights of making ends meet, or a freedom to look at a menu in a restaurant and choose what you want rather than what you can afford. It's a freedom from self-deprivation, and instead recognising that you are an amazing and abundant being.

I used to think that wealth was not for me because of where I came from, how I dressed and the fact that I hate brushing my hair. But it's actually for all of us.

Wealth is a material state for sure, but more than that it is a feeling. A beautiful and abundant feeling. You must first feel it to bring it into being. There are lots of things blocking you from your wealth, but the number one thing is your belief or lack of it.

I ran my first live event in September 2022 and one of the first things I asked my clients to do was to take a picture of themselves on their phone. All of these amazing women came together to learn more about money alchemy and manifesting with it, but this activity gave me wonderful goosebumps. Once they had taken the picture, I asked them to look at it and I told them 'This is what it looks like to be wealthy'. There were a lot of realisations in that moment, even though it was hard for some of them to see themselves as someone who could be wealthy.

Many of us think we have to change, to be more professional or wear smarter clothes, or, in my case brush my hair, to even have a chance at being wealthy. The truth is, wealthy people look just like you. Sure, some of them you can spot a mile off, but most are just normal people.

Remember that every time you look in the mirror or take a selfie... you are what a wealthy person looks like.

A common phrase I hear is 'I'll believe it when I see it', but the world of manifestation doesn't work that way. To see it, you have to believe it. Transforming into wealth starts with belief, and this will be followed by more and more evidence that you will discover.

Transforming into wealth isn't just your right. I believe it's a part of our duty, so that we can have even more impact on the world, and money alchemy will show you the way.

CHAPTER SUMMARY

- Wealth is first a feeling, then a reality.
- You may not notice the subtle shifts towards wealth.
- You don't need to change your appearance to become wealthy.
- Believe in wealth to see it.

IT'S TIME FOR A DIFFERENT WAY WITH MONEY

As I was writing this book, I had so many things to share with you about money and just how wonderful she is when you connect with her as a feminine being. My absolute passion and pleasure is showing you a different way of experiencing money.

We straddle the real world and magic realms and it's often easy to forget this when life happens and everyone around you is repeating similar things, habits around money specifically, but more generally, any type of magic. I know I went through a very long time in my life when I forgot how to dream, and I became more and more sceptical of the magic I'd seen as a girl.

The magic is always inside us, waiting to be seen. Sometimes you'll even get glimpses of it when you least expect it.

The magic of money alchemy is real. I live it daily and my clients do too. That doesn't mean it's easy to stick with the belief in it. The media, society and even friends and family members can make us doubt our ability to choose a different way.

Since I discovered money alchemy, my life has just felt so magical and blessed. I know that the more I build my connection and relationship with money, the more love and abundance I see all around me. Even when tough things happen in my life, this new faith in money keeps me calm and kind to myself. My mental health has improved and my income keeps on increasing. More than that, I'm happier in my own skin than ever before. I know that could be put down to my age now, but I truly believe that as women, we start returning to ourselves in our late thirties and that continues for us.

We're done with the ways we've been taught — there has to be more to life, right? And there is. Money alchemy is just one of the ways to lead you to more. More money yes, more abundance absolutely, but mostly more *you*, which is probably what you've always been looking for.

My mission is to be a part of the change that's needed in our world. To be part of the return to balance, which to me, means acknowledgement and acceptance that we are powerful and magical beings. To help the world move away from scarcity and towards abundance. I truly believe women with wealth and magic will bring about this change. Women like you.

BIBLIOGRAPHY

Here are the sources I've referred to in this book. All of them, I highly recommend you read. They will take you deeper into your healing journey and really support the transformation of your relationship with yourself and money.

Bodin , L., Bodin Lamboy, N. and Graciet, J. (2016) *The Book of Ho'oponopono: The Hawaiian Practice of Forgiveness and Healing*. Destiny Books.

Byrne, R. (2012) *The Magic*. Simon & Schuster Ltd.

Hamilton, D.R. (2021) *Why woo-woo works: The surprising science behind meditation, reiki, crystals, and other alternative practices*. Carlsbad, CA: Hay House.

Kondo, M. (2015) *The Life-Changing Magic of Tidying: The Japanese Art.* Vermilion.

Lister, L. (2017) Witch: *Unleashed. Untamed. Unapologetic.* Hay House UK Ltd

RESOURCES

I've mentioned several resources throughout this book and for ease, you can find them all in the link below:

- www.fearlesslyfeminine.me/book

I mentioned some of my gorgeous Money Magic Tools too so you might also like to check these out:

- Essence & Energy of Money Cards — a deck of 33 inspiring and connecting money affirmation cards.
www.fearlesslyfeminine.me/moneycards

Magical Manifestation Cheque Book — 50 cheques to create increases in your income month on month with full training.:

- www.fearlesslyfeminine.me/cheque

If you enjoyed this book and enjoy a good podcast too, have a listen to my Spiritual & Successful Podcast:

- www.fearlesslyfeminine.me/podcast

KEEP IN TOUCH

I'd love to hear all about your journey with money, so do stay in touch! There are several ways to do that.

If you'd love to carry on this gorgeous, positive conversation about money in a safe and supportive way, join my free group on Facebook.

- https://www.facebook.com/groups/moneymindsetforwomen-inbusiness

You can drop me an email:

- hello@fearlesslyfeminine.me

For more wonderful money information and tools there's my website:

- www.fearlesslyfeminine.me

If you'd like to roll up your sleeves in a fun and supportive group with me alongside you, join my next Free 5 Day Magnify Money Challenge:

- www.fearlesslyfemininine.me/challenge

WHAT'S NEXT?

I hope you've enjoyed this new way of being with money and are keen to try out some, or all, of the magical tools and techniques I've shared here.

If you'd like to dive even deeper into the concept of money as a feminine being and my magical money alchemy process, I have a powerful 16-week programme called Money Alchemy Academy

It's a deep dive into your specific and unique money personality and a journey to healing blocks, in a way that is perfect for you.

To find out more go to:

- www.fearlesslyfeminine.me/academymain

I'd love to see you there.

ACKNOWLEDGEMENTS

This book has been in me for several years and without several key people, would not have come into existence. First, I'd like to thank my coach Dan Meredith for pushing me, in just the right way, to get this written and boosting my confidence in general. Huge thanks go to Mark Jones, my partner, and soon to be husband. He sits quietly in my corner as our roots intertwine more each day. My son Cam, who doesn't know it, but has always been my driving force for being myself and finding a different way to inspire him. To my amazing team, clients and group members who keep me motivated to do even more and help them find their way too.

Printed in Great Britain
by Amazon

30332644R00119